THE ISLE OF MAN RAILWAY

A MODELLER'S INSPIRATION

Robin G. Winter

A **RAILWAY MODELLER** SPECIAL

Foreword

I feel privileged to have been asked to write the Foreword to this book about the Steam Railway on the Isle of Man – the island is indeed a magical place and those that know still raise their hand and say "Hello" to the fairies as they pass over the Fairy Bridge on the way from Douglas to Port Erin!

This book is a real inspiration to the railway modeller and enthusiast alike. Robin has tantalisingly described the different aspects of the Railway and its operations over the past 40 years or so. The modeller has so many choices whether it be the various types of locomotives and rolling stock or stations from the truly grand one at Douglas to a wayside halt such as Colby or Santon. From its base in the town of Douglas, the Railway runs through farmland, glens, past villages and small towns to end up in Port Erin, a friendly seaside resort with a sandy beach just five minutes walk from the station. There is plenty to inspire the modeller as will be seen from Robin's comprehensive and excellent selection of photographs.

As can be seen from the pictures, full signalling was provided at Douglas but, apart from the east end of St. John's on the erstwhile Peel line, signalling at the other stations was quite basic: a Home signal was provided from both directions at each station which controlled the trains' entrance. The authority to enter the next section was the driver having possession of the relevant train staff.

Some level crossings had Home signals but at others trains were flagged through by the Crossing Keeper.

As Robin mentions in this book, the Isle of Man Railway has gone through a lot of difficult times since the 1950s but at least the South line is still very much alive.

I first visited the Island in 1960 with my parents and I recall having breakfast in Douglas near the station after a somewhat rough overnight crossing from Liverpool. We travelled by steam train from St. Johns to Ramsey, Port Erin, and Peel, and it was magical!

Eight years later I returned for two sessions as a volunteer; amongst other duties, I was a Guard on the Douglas to Ramsey train. Then in 1969 I took up the post of Traffic Superintendent - cum - Stationmaster at Douglas. The following six years were both enjoyable and sad. It was enjoyable to be playing a part in the preservation of a wonderful old steam railway with a small but enthusiastic team who wanted the Railway to survive and thrive, but it was sad to see the Peel and Ramsey lines taken up and sold for scrap.

The Railway's future was indeed uncertain in the early 1970s but the efforts of the small nucleus of staff and supporters at that time played an important role - to my mind - in preserving the Railway for present and future generations to enjoy.

The Island is well worth a visit not only for the steam railway but also for the wealth of the other forms of rail transport.

Enjoy modelling the Isle of Man Railway!

Roger Webster

Contents

1	A brief history of the railway	6
	Portrait of a Duke	8
	Santon station, May 1953	12
2	Along the Port Erin line in the 1970s	14
	Douglas station	22
	South line centenary	23
	Short line working 1976	24
3	On shed at Douglas in the 1970s	26
4	Locomotives - origins and details	30
	New century, old livery	32
	The odd man out - *Caledonia*	36
5	Traces of the closed lines:	
	West to Peel	38
	Foxdale	43
	North to Ramsey	44
6	Signalling and permanent way	52
7	Signs of the times	58
8	The landscape and road traffic	60
9	Museum items and curios	68
10	Redundant locomotives	72
11	Internal combustion:	
	The railcars	76
	The diesel - *Viking*	79
12	Passenger vehicles	80
13	Freight stock	90
14	Liveries	94
	Paint guide - locos	100
	Paint guide - stock	102
15	Modelling	
	Port Foxdale layout	104
	Locomotives and rolling stock	112
	Bibliography and sources	130

ISBN 978 0 900586 95 8
A Railway Modeller Special. Edited by Andrew Burnham.
© 2007 Peco Publications & Publicity Ltd. Underleys, Beer, Seaton, Devon, EX12 3NA.

Printed by William Gibbons & Sons Ltd.,
P.O. Box 103, 26, Planetary Road, Willenhall, West Midlands, WV13 3XT.

Dedication

To my late mother, Audrey Rachel Edith, and father, Geoffrey, who in 1964 made the mistake of introducing me to the Isle of Man and its steam railway.

Also to my very patient and wonderful wife Susan, and our children Timothy and Annemarie, who have suffered my interest in the Isle of Man railway for so many years.

Introduction

In 1964, at the age of eight, I was introduced to a magnificent 3' gauge steam railway system, which at that time of course was larger than life and full of an atmosphere that I have not forgotten or encountered anywhere else since.

Douglas station had in those days a unique antiquated smell of smoke, oil, and coal dust. The platform-less stations around the system were something else, all different in character. Long fully loaded trains leaving Douglas, often with a locomotive at the rear to bank the train up the steep gradients.

The best bit of fun was watching the trains being put away at night. All the locomotives were painted Indian red livery in those days, with red and cream coaches.

In the 1970s when I returned to the island, things had changed dramatically. The last trains to St.John's, Peel, Kirk Michael, and Ramsey had all departed back in 1968.

The Peel departure platform, still with those magnificent glass and iron platform canopies, was filled with parked cars. On the Peel departure line stood several redundant locomotives, *Sutherland*, *Pender*, *Mannin*, *Thornhill*, and *Caledonia*.

Many of the photographs presented here were taken at that period in the 1970s. A lot of early mornings and patience spent in Douglas station and outside the locomotive shed meant that I was able to get pictures not normally possible for the travelling holidaymaker.

Locomotives No.4 *Loch* and No.13 *Kissack* in 'Ailsa' green feature in a lot of the photos purely because those two locos were the backbone of what was then known as the 'Victorian Steam Railway'.

I also had the privilege of travelling on the footplate of No.10 *G.H.Wood* on a permanent way train from Port St.Mary to Colby and back, a photographic delight. In addition, some time was spent cycling around the island photographing the remaining infrastructure of the closed lines.

Preface

One of the great things about the hobby of model railways is the diversity of other interests one encounters on the way to a finished working model.

I use the word 'finish' loosely because normally a model railway is never really finished, otherwise it becomes stale and uninteresting. We probably all have our own favourite areas in the construction of a layout - laying track, electrics, making the buildings and scenery, and the rolling stock - conversions from ready-to-run models, assembling kits, or scratchbuilding.

Research is probably my favourite and most time consuming pastime, one that I can spend hours on, looking through books, articles, and photographs, and carrying out site surveys. It is a continuous learning curve and improvement process. Whatever your favoured choice of railway company, period and style, research is invaluable.

This book not only offers a view of the Isle of Man Railway, mainly through the 1970s, but also a chance to observe the background not normally evident from the casual snapshot of an Isle of Man Railway train.

Above: Douglas station as it should be! Photographed from the signal box steps on a winter day c.1958. The locomotive in the centre is No.5 Mona. The time of year explains the lack of coaches in the yard to the right of the platforms, which on summer evenings after the day's services had ended would be packed. To the right of the central canopy which covered the Port Erin platform is the goods shed, which included a sunken siding. The full array of Dutton signals is apparent. The operating part of Douglas station today is virtually only half what can be seen here. Photo: Tony Hill collection.

I am particularly pleased that for a different perspective I have also been able to include many photos taken by David Odabashian in the mid-1950s. His coverage of the whole railway (with all but the Foxdale branch still fully working at that time) is remarkable for the period, and probably unparalleled.

Modellers should use many views of the same subject from several sources to create their own three-dimensional image of the item they wish to re-create, whether the aim is a precise replica or an interpretation in an individual style.

Within an inevitably limited number of pages, the coverage is both selective and personal. I hope reading it gives you as much pleasure as compiling it has given me.

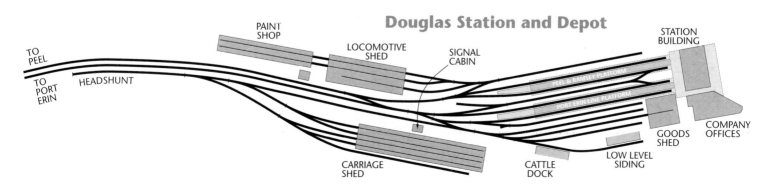

Douglas Station and Depot

TO PEEL
TO PORT ERIN
HEADSHUNT
PAINT SHOP
LOCOMOTIVE SHED
SIGNAL CABIN
CARRIAGE SHED
CATTLE DOCK
GOODS SHED
LOW LEVEL SIDING
PEEL & RAMSEY PLATFORM
PORT ERIN LINE PLATFORM
STATION BUILDING
COMPANY OFFICES

Chapter 1

A brief history of the railway

In the mid-1870s the Isle of Man recognised a new industry that had to be developed - tourism. It became apparent that means to transport visitors and locals alike around the island was required.

Millions of visitors have been to the island over many decades, but this business was to last less than a hundred years. The decline in visitors had a devastating effect on the island's economy and the railways after the Second World War.

The first of the 3' gauge railways was opened in 1873, coast to coast from Douglas to Peel, approximately ten miles in length. The three locomotives ordered for this new line were all 2-4-0 side tanks built by Beyer, Peacock in Manchester. Remarkably, the basic design of these little engines was to be retained by the IoMR until the last locomotive was purchased in 1926. Although improvements in power, water capacity, small working details, and general size were made, the whole fleet had a family appearance - Gorton style!

The passenger rolling stock in 1873 was three-compartment four-wheel stock; the first bogie stock arrived in 1876. Initial goods stock consisted of the popular M and H series open wagons and G vans.

1st August 1874 saw the opening of the south line to Port Erin, and the arrival of two more locomotives.

Buildings on the IoMR were generally cheap, simple, and effective, mostly of close boarded woodwork, to various designs, most with corrugated iron roofs. The exceptions

were Crosby and St.John's, which were Norwegian-style with tiled roofs. The wooden buildings on the Peel and Ramsey lines existed as built until well after the 1968 closures.

The first station at Douglas was also of wood construction but was later replaced with a grand stone and brick structure, like the other IoMR terminus buildings at Peel and Port Erin.

The building of railways on the island was not restricted to the IoMR. In 1879 the Manx

Above: after 125 years, No.1 Sutherland *is still an icon of the railway. It is seen here returning to the running shed in Douglas in the summer of 1998. The sloping smokebox is very noticeable. This early Beyer, Peacock characteristic gives the loco a quaint appearance compared to the more conventionally shaped later locos.*

Northern Railway opened a line from Ramsey down the northwest coast of the island to St.John's. This concern had its own terminus at St.John's and a fleet of six-wheel Cleminson composite coaches and locomotives from Sharp, Stewart and Dübs & Co.

Architecture on this line was far more substantial with Peel red sandstone station buildings and some extremely expensive civil engineering in the form of two stone and wrought-iron viaducts across Glen Mooar and Glen Wyllin, rebuilt by the IoMR around 1920.

In 1886 the final 3' gauge line to be built on the island was opened from St.John's to Foxdale, serving the lead mines in that area. Only 2½ miles long on a 1 in 49 gradient, this line handled the mines' products and spoil, and coal in return. A limited passenger service also existed but only until around 1940.

Left: hundreds of people leaving a packed Kirk Braddan 'Sunday Special' on its return to Douglas. One of the noticeable features of this picture is that whilst the passengers are still pouring off the train, there is no locomotive attached. Up to the 1970s, it was normal procedure for the loco crews to waste no time in detaching the engine from the train and returning to the shed as quickly as possible.
Photo: the late David Odabashian.

Having absorbed the failing Manx Northern Railway in 1905, the IoMR was now operating some 46 route miles of railway on an island only 10 miles wide by 33 miles long. 1905 also saw the arrival of the first of the locomotives built with a large 3'3" diameter boiler, No.10 *G.H.Wood*. Some of the earlier locos were to receive replacement larger boilers and side tanks during their working lives.

Track ballast was always taken from local sources and the pits at St.John's. Spoil from the mines at Foxdale was also used and it is interesting to note that, because of the lead content, track ballasted with this rarely had a weed to be seen.

The IoMR track had flat bottom rail spiked to half-round sleepers and was buried in ballast to rail level, whilst the MNR employed more conventional methods.

The type of visitor changed in 1914 when the whole of Isle of Man was turned into an internment camp during the First World War. Military and prisoner-of-war trains were part of the normal daily traffic. A new short branch was built off the Peel line to Knockaloe where a p-o-w camp was built. No.4 *Caledonia* operated the line. This line even boasted its own engine shed which can still be seen on Knockaloe Farm.

In 1926 the last of the fifteen Beyer, Peacock locomotives arrived, No.16 *Mannin* - the largest of the fleet and the most powerful at the time, built for the heavy south line services.

The railway's heyday could be considered as being between the two world wars. In the summer months, trains of fourteen or more coaches could be seen full of holidaymakers, especially on the Port Erin line. Many trains had to be banked out of Douglas up the gradient through Nunnery and Oakhill cuttings into Port Soderick. The engine at the rear then dropped off and returned light to Douglas light, probably to do the same for the next service.

The length of the passing loops at some of the stations bears witness to the length of trains. However, it was not unknown for some trains to consist of just one coach even in high season, for example on the Foxdale branch or even the shuttle service from St.John's to Peel. In the winter the service was reduced almost to one loco and coach for the whole system. The railcars were used after 1961.

The north line to Ramsey did not always experience such great length trains; one or two coaches often sufficed. Common practice was for Ramsey and Peel trains to leave Douglas coupled together in one rake and double headed; they divided at St.John's in quite a unique way. Part of the train was literally left stranded on the main line outside of the station until the loco returned from the front portion of the train it had deposited in the station.

These split trains would often unofficially leave St.John's same time, instead of the booked two minute difference, as the Ramsey and Peel lines out of St.John's were two separate single lines running parallel and the promise of a good race could not be resisted! The Peel train generally won as the Ramsey route was uphill. Several of Ivo Peters' Manx films show this practice well - in fact, on occasions this 'race' was obviously done to order.

The open-air church services at Kirk Braddan were very popular and on summer Sunday mornings virtually every coach was used to convey visitors to Braddan station, approximately two miles outside Douglas on the Peel line. The term station should be used lightly, as it was no more than a hut and a lengthy section of gravel for a platform. Trains would be emptied and travel on to Union Mills for engines to run round and return to Braddan.

Some seventy-five bogie and fourteen six-wheel Cleminson coaches of differing designs and sizes were used on the island, the last arriving in 1926. In addition to the purpose-built bogie coaches, the IoMR had been placing the bodies of old four-wheel stock in pairs on new bogie chassis: known as the 'pairs', some still exist in service today.

Above: No.1 Sutherland *in charge of a rake of four coaches in 1998 crosses Nunnery Bridge at the beginning of the 1 in 65 gradient uphill to Oakhill and Port Soderick. This gradient was the reason that the long trains of the railway's heyday needed banking by an engine at the rear. Trains would leave Douglas with some speed and make an effort to get a good run at the slope.*

The chassis from the old four-wheeled coaches were not wasted: they were converted into freight vehicles.

Although the IoMR had quite a fleet of freight vehicles, dedicated goods trains were not a normal sight except maybe on certain market days and during the two world wars. Generally what needed to travel got attached to the back of a passing passenger train.

Although not lifted, the Foxdale branch was closed to passenger traffic in 1940, and the odd train continued to traverse the line to clear the spoil heaps until 1960.

Below: beginning between the wars, then more so in the 1950s, bus and road competition took an enormous amount of business away from all railways. The Isle of Man Railway took the bold step of buying out the bus companies to control the competition. In this June 1954 view of the old Port Erin bus depot, across the top of open wagon M50 we see a railway-owned 32-seat Bedford OWB of 1945, with Duple utility saloon bodywork, in Isle of Man Road Services livery. Photo: the late David Odabashian.

Below: No.3 Pender *shunting at Port Erin in June 1954. Freight traffic was already being lost to road vehicles, and the G van may have been for fish, or to be added to a passenger working to cater for luggage. On the siding in the background a spare coach waits to strengthen a regular service train when required.*
Photo: the late David Odabashian.

Portrait of a Duke

Built at Beyer, Peacock's Gorton Foundry in Manchester in 1873, this was the first of fifteen engines that the company was eventually to build for the Isle of Man. It was named after the Third Duke of Sutherland, the company's first Chairman.

One of the three locos delivered for the opening, No.1 *Sutherland* was withdrawn from service in 1964 with a weak boiler. It went on display at St.John's and Douglas before entering the Port Erin museum in 1975.

In 1996 it was removed from the museum and taken to the workshops in Douglas, where the locomotive was beautifully restored to the condition we see here. *Sutherland* rejoined the serviceable fleet on 2nd May 1998 in time for the Isle of Man Railway's 125th anniversary.

However, it had been rebuilt with a boiler temporarily borrowed from No.8 *Fenella* which should have been returned to that locomotive in 2002, though in fact it was not until 2003. *Sutherland* will be returned to the museum.

Above: Sutherland *in a sylvan setting at Castletown on a southbound service in 1998.*

Right: in 2001, all the serviceable locomotives were repainted into an Indian red livery, though this differs in some small respects from the post-war scheme - the cab footstep rear plates are painted to match the rest of the loco; previously they were painted black. Sutherland *is seen here at the back of the running shed in front of F39, the Foxdale coach, during August 2001.*

During the Second World War, the railway must have taken quite a bashing with little if any maintenance being done.

In this period some locos appeared in Brunswick green without lining when and if any painting was done. Some locos never recovered from the extensive war use and many other items of stock were simply worn out and laid to rest, never to be used again.

In 1946/7 a new image for the railway was announced, although not carried out with any haste. The change of livery for the locos was to the now famous and well-loved Indian red with yellow-black-yellow lining, with red and cream coaches. Some of the 'pairs' and Cleminson coaches were painted in a red-brown livery.

After the war, the number of cars on the island was to increase with more people travelling by road than by train. Visitor numbers also declined dramatically. As elsewhere, this had an effect on the railway. So instead of the return to its heyday business, timetables were reduced and many other cost-cutting measures were carried out. By the late 1950s the railway business was in serious decline with no apparent future.

Two railcars from the closed County Donegal Joint Railways Committee were purchased in 1961 to help keep operating costs down. Economies and withdrawal of services continued until 1965 when the railway finally closed. Posters were placed advising the need for essential track maintenance.

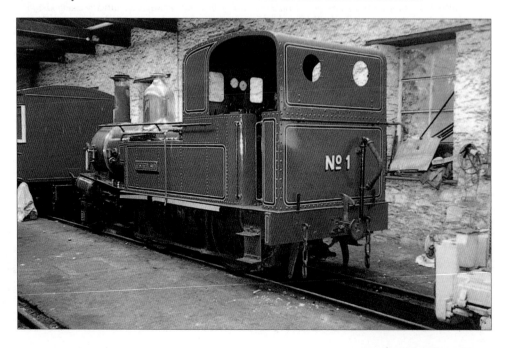

Above: Sutherland *is seen simmering at Port Erin during the summer of 1998, unmistakably a product of the Beyer, Peacock company. The green livery applied to the loco after its overhaul was slightly darker than the original 'Ailsa' green used in the 1960s and 1970s.*

No trains at all ran in 1966 and everybody thought the railway was lost.

The Marquis of Ailsa leased the whole system in 1967 and the lines opened for business in the summer of that year. However, because of the decline in services and deferral of repairs, only seven out of the original sixteen locomotives were serviceable - No.5 *Mona*, No.8 *Fenella*, No.10 *G.H. Wood*, No.11 *Maitland*, No.12 *Hutchinson*, No.13 *Kissack*, and No.15 *Caledonia* - which had been little used by the old company - as well as the 'new' railcars.

However, by the end of 1968 No.5 *Mona*, No.8 *Fenella*, and No 15. *Caledonia* were all to be withdrawn due to weak boilers. No.5 has never returned to steam whilst No.15 was not restored until 1994 and No.8 did not return to traffic until 2003.

The working engines together with a number of unusable locos put out on display were painted in a new light green livery, similar to LNER Doncaster green, with white-black-white lining; this came to be known as 'Ailsa' green.

The coaches remained in the post-war red and cream.

Redundant No.14 *Thornhill*, No.16 *Mannin*, No.3 *Pender*, No.1 *Sutherland* and eventually No.15 *Caledonia* could be seen in a line up at St.John's and after closure of the Peel line they were displayed at Douglas station. No.6 *Peveril* and No.9 *Douglas* were nowhere to be seen. It was generally accepted that these locomotives were worn out: No.1 and No.3 certainly had extremely wasted boilers, while No.16 still had its original 1926 boiler and required at least a replacement if nothing else. No.15, used in 1967 in 'Ailsa' green, was soon painted in an MNR type livery in 1968 and then caused many steaming problems for the crews. No.14 had been withdrawn in 1964 again with a weak boiler.

In 1967/8 Lord Ailsa made an attempt to encourage new freight business with the introduction of an oil tanker service from Peel to a power station at Ramsey, and a container service between Douglas and Castletown. Neither lasted after the 1968 closures.

On 6th September 1968 the Ramsey line closed forever with the Peel line following the day after. Interestingly, the day the Peel line closed, the major overhaul of No.4 *Loch* was finished, complete with a new Hunslet boiler. The loco was run in on the Peel line.

The three closed lines (Peel, Ramsey, and Foxdale) were not lifted until 1975 along with much of the main infrastructure. Many coaches were left in store at St.John's and were lost through vandalism or demolition.

The surviving south line has not been short of knocks; the early 1970s saw only four departures each day from Douglas to Port Erin, Monday to Friday, with no service on Saturdays and only five serviceable locomotives. In 1975 the line was closed between Douglas and Castletown, although in 1976 it was extended back to Ballasalla.

Fortunately the whole line was re-opened in 1977 under government ownership and seems to have improved ever since - an interesting role reversal as now the authorities that ran the buses also ran the trains. Coaching stock remained in red and cream with the exception of the saloons which were eventually painted all-over coach red. Such locos as were available for service were still in 'Ailsa' green.

The 1980s and 1990s saw many special events take place with locomotives being taken from the museum and restored to service, different historical liveries used, and locos turned to run bunker-first from Douglas. There was also a revival of double-headed trains, and *Caledonia* even worked on Snaefell Mountain.

The 1990s also saw the acquisition of a four-wheel diesel locomotive, No.17, named *Viking*.

It is unlikely we shall ever see trains to Peel or Ramsey on the old IoMR routes but one line is better than none and what is left is a tribute to what was a fine railway system. The appointment of David Howard as Director of Transport (1992 - 2006) saw the welcome return of the old company corporate image and one can now appreciate something of the atmosphere the railway once had in the 1940s and 1950s, even if there is only half a station in Douglas.

There was once a very noticeable time lapse on the island: the speed of normal life was quite different from the UK, much slower. This cannot be said of the Isle of Man today. In terms of moving around and public transport

in the 1960s and 1970s, for example, you could always guarantee seeing much older road vehicles, which were no longer in use on the mainland and would have been considered collectors' items, but here they were a normal part of daily life. Douglas Corporation Transport and the Isle of Man Road Services, the two bus companies, seemed to run types of vehicles that had been long replaced elsewhere. The railway company had delivery vans and lorries out of the ark. This is brilliant for modelling, as it enables you to mix styles from different decades, and this is what gives the Isle of Man some of its magic.

Since 2000, raised platforms have been added to stations on the Port Erin line; not the least benefit of these is in terms of improved disabled access to the trains. It is also intended to convert a number of coaches so that every train can have provision for wheelchairs.

The controversial 'bus stop' shelters are out of character for the old IoMR railway. I suppose the Manx taxpayers who are paying for the railway and who need to be encouraged back to using it deserve some relief from the weather, but it is just a shame that replica IoMR buildings could not be funded.

Another of the many sad decisions is that all the original IoMR wooden crossing gates have gone in favour of modern lifting barriers. Safety measures are now understandably very strict on road crossings and essentially it is a case of installing automatic lifting barriers or no railway. The other distraction is that of staff wearing high-visibility vests!

This is all in contrast to some of the stories of the old IoMR. The railway was not subject to the British Board of Trade and despite having a rule book many operating practices were regularly employed that would not meet Health & Safety requirements today! Though it must be noted that not one passenger was injured or lost their life in the entire history of the Isle of Man Railway Company.

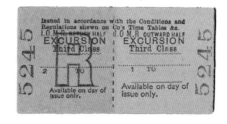

Railway time line - a brief chronology

1873

IoMR opened between Douglas and Peel, via Union Mills, Crosby, and St.John's. Three locomotives available for opening: No.1 *Sutherland*, No.2 *Derby*, and No.3 *Pender*.

1874

IoMR line from Douglas to Port Erin opened, through Port Soderick, Santon, Ballasalla, Castletown (then the capital of the island), Colby Level, and Port St.Mary. Two further locomotives were delivered, No.4 *Loch* and No.5 *Mona*.

1876

Proposal to build a railway north from Greeba (on the Peel line) to Ramsey via Glen Helen and Ballaugh and then on to what became the Manx Northern route into Ramsey. The scheme was presented again in 1884, and failed again.

1876

Proposal to build a line from Peel (not the IoMR station) to Glen Helen and on via the above route by the newly-formed Manx Northern Railway company.

1877

Proposed route to Jurby and Andreas in the north of the island.

1879

Manx Northern Railway opened, from St.John's (West) to St.Germains, Kirk Michael, Ballaugh, Sulby Glen, Sulby Bridge, and Lezayre. The MNR line was operated by the IoMR from 23rd September 1879 to 6th November 1880

1881

First trains from Ramsey on the MNR allowed onto IoMR metals through to Douglas. Coaches were normally attached to the rear of IoMR trains at St.John's.

1882/3

IoMR proposed route from Ballaleece on the Peel line east of St.John's to Foxdale and then on to St.Marks and Castletown or Ballasalla.

1883

MNR Ramsey quay railway completed.

1886

Foxdale Railway opened, being operated on a lease to the MNR. The line ran down through Waterfall, over the IoMR line at St.John's to the MNR station at St.John's (West), on a 1 in 49 gradient throughout.

1888

A repeat of the 1885 proposal for a branch from St.John's to Glen Helen. St.Germains station closed on the opening of Peel Road Station.

1888

MNR proposal to run a branch from Peel Road (Poortown) to Peel failed.

1899

Manx Electric Railway completed from Douglas to Ramsey; this affected business on the MNR and IoMR.

1905

Manx Northern and Foxdale routes absorbed into Isle of Man Railway ownership. All locomotives and coaches were taken into IoMR ownership, but not all were used.

1912

MNR loco. No.2 *Northern* broken up in Douglas.

1914

First World War, visitor traffic slumped but significant increase in freight traffic by 1915. Much traffic generated by H.M. forces.

1915

Knockaloe Branch near Peel built by IoMR to internment camp. A branch was built along the quayside at Peel, but removed after the war.

1917

A new livery for coaches: tan upper and chocolate lower panels.

1918-21

Knockaloe Branch closed, Glen Wyllin and Glen Mooar viaducts rebuilt.

1923

Knockaloe Branch lifted. MNR No.1 *Ramsey* broken up in Douglas.

1925

Ransome and Rapier turntable installed at St.John's, 35' diameter with 55 ton capacity. Built by Ransome and Rapier for the West Clare Railway, it was never delivered to that concern and was offered to the IoMR. It was not to turn engines but rolling stock to allow for equal wear and weathering.

1926

Last steam locomotive built and delivered by Beyer, Peacock (No.16 *Mannin*).
St.Germains station re-opened.

1929

IoMR purchased both the island's bus operators, Manx Motors and Isle of Man Road Services.

1935

The Isle of Man Railway Company purchased the Glen at Glen Wyllin a few hundred yards from Kirk Michael station. The railway made provision for a boating lake, refreshments, children's playground and other attractions. Trains introduced to run from Douglas and terminate at Kirk Michael.

1938

Colby Level, Ballabeg, Peel Road, and St.Germains became request halts for certain trains only.

1939

Outbreak of Second World War. Despite no holiday-makers, the railway saw significant increase in traffic related to internment camps, with P.o.W. and military movements, etc. New RAF bases were constructed at Jurby and Andreas (north line, nearest station Sulby Bridge) and Ronaldsway (south line, Ballasalla or Castletown).

1940

Foxdale line closed permanently to passengers. Mineral movements continued in large quantities for the construction of roads and runways. This continued for many years after the war.

1945

No.7 *Tynwald* became the first loco to be dismantled due to economies and a lack of spare parts, though never officially scrapped. All rolling stock was in poor condition, some wagons worn out and beyond repair.

1944/5

New livery of Indian red for locomotives and red and cream for coaches. It was a slow transition!

1945/6

Visitor numbers were slow to return to pre-war numbers, and the inter-war boom was not to return. Locomotive fleet in poor condition. Further engines taken out of service and stored or used as sources of parts.

1950

Large decline in summer visitors and services due to increase in foreign holidays. Port Erin line still managed some heavy trains. Second locomotive scrapped for parts, No.2 *Derby*.

1952

Ramsey quay line closed.

1957

Winter services reduced to a minimum.
Two diesel railcars purchased from C.D.J.R.C, soon painted all-over coach red with cream waistline strip.
Last train on Foxdale line (except for spoil trains).

1961

Winter services on the St.John's - Peel section suspended.

1962

Summer services reduced to six each way Port Erin, five to six each way to Peel, and two only each way to Ramsey. Winter services on the Ramsey line suspended.

1963

Winter services consisted of one daily trip only over each line with just a locomotive and one coach, or the railcars.

Opposite left: No.5 Mona *on a Port Erin train at Port Soderick, August 1955.*
Opposite right: No.8 Fenella *with a train for Ramsey at St.John's, July 1956.*

Above left: No.3 Pender *waits at Peel with a train for Douglas, July 1956.*
Above: No.4 Loch *at Castletown with a train for Port Erin , August 1955.*

1965
Significant collapse of passenger traffic, all services were suspended in November.

1966
Whole railway remained closed all year. Track in very poor condition.

1967
The railway was leased by the IoMR to Lord Ailsa under a 20 year agreement. All lines re-opened for summer services. New light green livery for locomotives. Some redundant locomotives displayed at St.John's. A container service from Castletown and oil tank trains from Peel to Milntown (Ramsey) began: it was not a success and did not continue after 1968. Ronaldsway Halt opened between Ballasalla and Castletown.

1968
Another very poor year for visitors to the island.The Ramsey line closed to passengers on 8th September, though the oil workings continued for a further few months. The Peel line closed completely on 7th September, but No.4 *Loch* returned to service on the same day with a new boiler.

1969
Formation of the Isle of Man Victorian Steam Railway Co.Ltd. to operate the only existing line, to Port Erin, with minimum of four trains each way but no trains on Saturdays, a situation that lasted for many years. Staff wore Victorian costume. April saw the last of the oil workings on the north line to Ramsey, thus closing it completely.

1972
The original Isle of Man Railway Company resumed control with a subsidy from the Manx government tourist board.

1973
IoMR centenary year.

1974
The Peel, Ramsey, and Foxdale lines were sold for scrap and were lifted along with demolition of many buildings and bridges. Also scrapped were historic items of rolling stock still in the carriage shed at St.John's. Redundant locos were put on display in Douglas station whilst No.5 *Mona* was shown at Port Erin. Others were stored in a state of disrepair. Redundant historic stock broken up at Ballasalla during November.

1975
Withdrawal of Government subsidy resulted in short line working only between Castletown and Port Erin. Douglas station was put up for sale.

1976
Railway operations moved closer to Douglas with the line from Ballasalla to Port Erin running.

1977
Full line operations resumed between Douglas and Port Erin.The railcars were repainted into the coach livery of black roof, cream above the waistline, and red below waistline.

1978
The Isle of Man Railway Company was sold to the Manx government.The services and operation were to be managed by the Manx Electric Railway Board.

1979
No.3 *Pender* of 1873 was sold to the Museum of Science and Industry in Manchester, whilst No.6 *Peveril* was to be loaned to the National Railway Museum in York. In fact it never left the island.

1981
'New' livery for the coaches: the purple lake of the Manx Northern. With one exception the existing loco fleet was painted in what were termed 'historical' liveries. Locomotives available for service at this time were No.4 *Loch*, No.11 *Maitland*, No.12 *Hutchinson* and No.13 *Kissack*.

1982
The railcars and some saloon coaches were painted into the now nationalised bus company colours of red and white.

1990
Railcars now in very poor condition and unsuitable for passenger use.

1992/93
German-built diesel purchased, given No.17 and named *Viking*. No.15 *Caledonia* returned to service after some 20 years, and operated services on Snaefell Mountain in connection with that railway's centenary. No.10 *G.H.Wood* returned to service.

1997
Restoration of ex-CDR railcars begun.

1998
No.1 *Sutherland* of 1873 returned to traffic for IoMR 125th Anniversary.

1998/9
Douglas Station site reduced by half, including removal of Port Erin platforms, canopies, carriage shed. Douglas Signal box moved to new site adjacent to new running line. New carriage shed built next to Peel line formation behind existing workshops. Carriage shed commissioned at Port Erin. Some stations received platforms which historically never had them - Castletown, Ballasalla, Colby, Ronaldsway, and a second platform at Port Soderick.

2000
Locomotives painted Indian red, coaches returned to red and cream. Santon station fully restored including provision of platforms.

2001
No.15 *Caledonia* painted in GER style dark blue livery. Brightly coloured bus shelters appeared on Castletown and Ballasalla stations. Kewaigie railway bridge over the Douglas to Castletown road just south of Douglas rebuilt to allow for heavier and larger road traffic.

2001-3
Parts of Port Erin line closed in order to lay pipeline from Meary Veg (south of Crogga Wood) to Port Erin. This resulted in new track throughout from Douglas to Port Erin, including replacement of all original IoMR crossing gates with automatic train-operated lifting barriers.

2002
New stone clad overbridge built at the south end of Crogga Woods.

2003
No.1 *Sutherland* withdrawn, and with an uncertain future. No.8 *Fenella* returns to service after a 35-year gap. Platform installed at Colby level crossing! Railway purchases its first mechanical tamping machine.

2004
Hunslet four-wheeled diesel loco used by pipeline and track contractors, originally built for the Channel Tunnel and London's Jubilee Line extension projects, is purchased by Isle of Man Transport, given the number18 and named *Ailsa*; it is currently painted white.

2005
No.13 *Kissack* returned to service after a gap of 14 years, having donated its original boiler to No.10 in 1991. Non-prototypical semaphore signals installed at Douglas station. Ballabeg halt given platform.
Last remaining standing IoMR Linley & Co. slotted signal at Castletown is brought to the ground in a storm.

2006
Largest number of locomotives available for service for many decades, eight in total: Nos. 4 *Loch*, 8 *Fenella*, 10 *G.H.Wood*, 11 *Maitland*, 12 *Hutchinson*, 15 *Caledonia*, 17 *Viking*, and 18 *Ailsa*. The passenger fleet numbers just ten serviceable coaches.

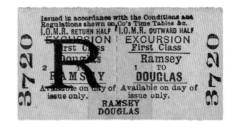

Santon

What better way to while away the time while waiting for your train on a fine spring day than to observe and record the station and its surroundings? On 30th May 1953, David Odabashian did just that, providing us with a time capsule portrait of a typical IoMR wayside station.

Little was to change until this sole surviving section of the system was substantially rebuilt in the 1990s - the track was renewed, the station got a proper platform, and the stone plinth on which the old van body that served as the goods shed had stood became an ornamental flower bed.

Top: No.5 Mona *arrives in charge of a northbound service from Port Erin to Douglas.*

Above and left: the station building, constructed of matchboarding on a timber frame, with a corrugated iron roof. The toilet block was brick-built.

Above: the long advertising hoarding, constructed of timber panelling supported by old rails. The IoMR built such screens to conceal 'unsightly' goods facilities from those travelling to enjoy the landscape.

Right: looking towards Port Erin past the station sign and goods platform.

Below left: the goods shed from the road side.

Below right: the view from the platform side, the large advertising hoarding masking the goods siding starts immediately to the right of the gas lamp.

The station site was fully described, with additional photos showing the current situation, complete with a track plan and layout suggestion, in the June 2006 RAILWAY MODELLER.

Chapter 2

Along the Port Erin line in the 1970s

Many of the photographs in this book follow the Port Erin line as that was the part of the Isle of Man Railway that was left working after the 1968 closures, and they therefore form a pictorial record of the final years under the ownership of the Isle of Man Railway Company as such, before nationalisation.

Lord Ailsa had come and gone, and large expenditure was still required but not available. The Peel and Ramsey lines had closed forever, although in the early 1970s some of the closed railway sites and stations still looked as if they were waiting for the next train to arrive.

At this time all the locos in service were still painted in the bright apple green livery introduced by Lord Ailsa. Some of the redundant locomotives on display at Douglas still carried the old Indian red, and *Caledonia*, No.15 or No.4, according to which company you prefer, was in Manx Northern Railway red, whilst No.5 *Mona*, a favourite loco of mine, was on show at Port Erin station in a very dull 'Ailsa' green.

Coaches were still in the red and cream post-war livery. The remaining goods stock was scattered about the system in all sorts of greys, some paint bare and some being held together by fresh air and well-rusted iron work.

In the early 1970s, few trains if any ran on Saturdays, but on certain Sunday afternoons

one could travel to Port Erin on the 14.10 from Douglas, then join an express service from Port Erin to Castletown on a return special, the '*Castletown Flyer*', all before tea back in Douglas.

The mid-1970s were again very uncertain times. By 1975 the situation worsened and the surviving line was again truncated, running only from Castletown to Port Erin, though Ballasalla won a reprieve in 1976. The great ornate Victorian gates at Douglas station remained firmly closed, only the movement of stock needing access to the works for servicing could be seen.

Above: No.12 Hutchinson *in the release road on the original Port Erin platform at Douglas with the fireman operating the points. I always marvelled at the speed with which the loco crews uncoupled the loco from its train at any of the terminus stations. It seemed as if there was a race to return the loco to the sheds after use - or was it just the call of the mess coach and the teapot?!*

The Manx Peacocks varied in many details, and this example is just one. Only two of the fifteen Beyer, Peacock locomotives carried their numbers on the tank sides above the nameplate. No.5 Mona *had a 5" brass number on the left-hand tank only, mounted on a green plaque, whilst No.12 had the number on both tank sides but on a black painted plaque.*

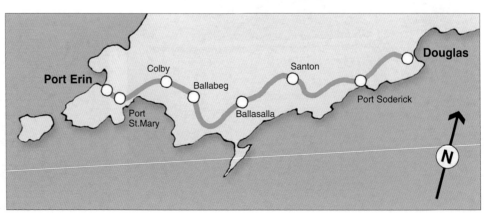

Right: No.11 Maitland *was built along with No.10* G.H.Wood *in 1905, and is seen at Douglas in the 'Victorian Steam Railway' period in the 1970s when all the service trains carried ornate lamps on the front buffer beam.*

With the exception of 1975/6 when the railway was only running between Port Erin and Castletown or Ballasalla, I do not think I have ever visited the island without seeing this stalwart at work.

There were many differences between the fourteen Beyer,Peacocks and probably the most noticeable here is the polished brass cover around the base of the safety valve casing on this loco. Before 1967 this brass cover was on No.13 Kissack. Other locos have this casing painted.

Below: No.12 Hutchinson *in Douglas station in 1974. The vehicle behind the loco is one of the older 'pairs' coaches. They were fun to ride in, despite being very sparse in terms of comfort. Sadly, many of these vehicles no longer exist, except for a number of underframes in permanent way use.*

Below left: 1910-built No.13 Kissack, *one of only five serviceable locomotives in the 1970s, shunting at the Port Erin platform at Douglas on a very wet morning in 1973. There is much of interest - the trackwork, so different to the present layout at Douglas, is well buried in ash up to rail level, the normal practice in the old IoMR days. The fine array of Dutton signals have now long gone, with the signal box and iron carriage shed in the background. A wooden stage once stood between the water columns, with baskets of coal for the locos.*

Below: No.13 Kissack *again, this time on a somewhat drier day, leaving for Port Erin, framed by the now redundant signals that once adorned the departure roads at Douglas.*

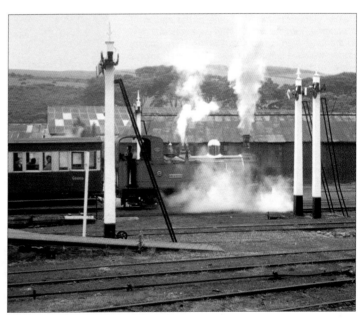

Left: No.4 Loch leaving Crogga Woods, just south of Port Soderick, travelling north, bound for Douglas. Those interested in authentic modelling will note the state of the lineside fencing and gates!

Right: No.4 again, this time passing under Mill Road bridge south of Castletown on its way to Port Erin. Note the fireman is standing on the edge of the cab side. When the cab floors and bunkers were full of coal there was not much room left for the crew.

Below: Santon Bank, just south of the station of that name, with the first up train on a very dull day. In the long, high curving bank is the Fairy Bridge, under which a stream flows. One must always show respect to the fairies when crossing this bridge - a simple "Hello", "Good morning", or "Good afternoon" is sufficient to prevent bad luck!

Four more views of No.4 Loch travelling along the Port Erin line.

Above: at Ballasalla in front of the tiny corner crossing gatehouse which houses the wheel for the gates only. In the 1970s Ballasalla still had its Class Three timber and tin roof station building, The decorative ornate Victorian lamps on the front of the loco were seen on most if not all trains during this period.

Right: leaving Castletown travelling north, in the cutting just beyond the station. A wealth of detail can be observed in this photo - the sunken state of the weed-covered permanent way, with some rotting sleepers, and the overgrown foliage which is creeping towards the track on the embankment. The wild fuchsias on the left are quite a common sight by the track on the Isle of Man.

Below: entering Castletown during 1974. Note the tank patches, which varied from one loco to another, almost to the extent that one could identify a loco just by them.

Below right: at Port St.Mary in 1976 with a northbound train, which includes one of the saloons in the all-red livery of the period.

Left: No.4 Loch travelling at speed over Four Roads level crossing. Note the colour of the crossing lady's flag. In this photo it is yellow, but the old IoMR rule book indicates that it should normally have been a white 'all clear' signal flag. Train guards also used the white flag. A green flag would be used to start a train, and immediately the train left the station the white 'all clear' flag would be shown. The driver would acknowledge this with a short whistle. This was originally to show that each trainman was at his post and the guard and brakemen had not been left behind. The Marquis of Ailsa sought to change this rule, as "too many children wave white handkerchiefs"! However, I can still remember white flags being used in 1974.

Below: No.10 G.H.Wood at the rear of the first down train of the morning at Port St.Mary. This loco had been attached as a banking engine from Douglas and ran through for the purpose of permanent way duties at Port Erin but, believe me, it had worked its passage as much as the train engine. It always seemed a very vocal loco.

Above: dedicated freight trains were not a common sight on the IoMR, even in the old company days. Most freight was loaded onto a van or wagon and attached to the next passenger train in the appropriate direction. Lord Ailsa attempted a freight revival in the 1960s, with oil tankers and a 'Man-tainor' service, neither of which survived very long.

These three photos show a permanent way train. No.10 G.H.Wood had travelled down on the tail of the 10.10 departure from Douglas to Port Erin and was detached at Port St.Mary where it collected these two M wagons from the yard having let the service train go on to Port Erin. I was lucky enough to be invited onto the footplate and travelled from Port St.Mary to Colby and then back to Port Erin with this train - an experience I shall never forget.

Above right: just north of Four Roads crossing, staff get down to business on a gully clearing exercise. This was a rather pungent moment!

Right: once finished, we reversed up the line to Colby station to enable a north-bound service train to pass.

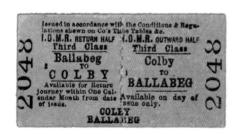

Above left: outside Port Erin shed we see No.11 Maitland, simmering and waiting for the return working. An old coach chassis converted into a runner, a G van, and an unidentified passenger coach sit on the goods shed siding. The water tank and tower have been rebuilt since this photo was taken; the new structure is much smaller.

Left: No.4 Loch outside Port Erin shed during the short line years, in 1976. Note the 'scratchbuilt' coaling stage.

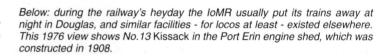

Below: No.4 Loch outside Port Erin shed. Loch received a new boiler in 1968, the same year the Peel and Ramsey lines closed; the boiler was supplied by Hunslet, as Beyer,Peacock had ceased trading in 1965. Loch was returned to traffic in 'Ailsa' green.

Below: during the railway's heyday the IoMR usually put its trains away at night in Douglas, and similar facilities - for locos at least - existed elsewhere. This 1976 view shows No.13 Kissack in the Port Erin engine shed, which was constructed in 1908.

Above: Port Erin, terminus of the south line. No.4 Loch has arrived and is running round to be serviced before departure. The station building is the second on the site, a Ruabon red brick building with timber and glass canopy. It is little changed from when it was built in 1905. There are some very ornate carvings in the gables that are repeated throughout the building. Platforms were added to match the other termini in 1914. The arrangement is peculiar as there is a public right of way across the centre, and the 650' platform, which could take a fourteen coach train, dips in the centre for the roadway, as seen in the view below.

Right: No.11 Maitland awaits its next departure north during the summer of 1974. Note that at this period the platform still had its cast iron railings around the station boundary. The bay platforms that had for decades been in regular use both for departures and for storage of coaching stock were now filled in and used for storing buses.

Below: No.4 Loch waiting for the off at Port Erin.

Left: a depressing sight in 1975/1976 when for the second time in its history Douglas station was closed for two seasons. But for the intervention of Tynwald, Douglas station could very well have closed forever at the end of the 1974 season, despite the euphoria of the centenary celebrations only a year earlier. Although closed in 1975/6 it was still complete, unlike today - the glass and iron canopies were still there, the Port Erin arrival and departure platforms, as well as platforms for the now closed Peel and Ramsey lines, plus the locomotive works, a working signal box, signals, and a corrugated iron carriage shed - in fact, everything you would expect at a major railway station, except a train service!

Left: Douglas station forecourt during the 'Victorian Steam Railway' period. Note the Victorian lady on the station tower roof.

Below: the magnificent view from Athol Street of the grand entrance to Douglas station with its gold leaf pillars and entrance gates.

THE ISLE OF MAN RAILWAY

Above: one year after the celebrations to mark one hundred years since the opening of the Peel line, 1st August 1974 saw the centenary of the south line, Douglas to Port Erin. One special train was run in the afternoon, complete with a banking engine. It was an excuse to give the flags and shield an airing, as seen (right) on No.4 Loch prior to departure of the 10.10 service to Port Erin.

Below: the booking office within Douglas station building, in 1974. It is interesting that first class travellers to Peel and Ramsey once had the use of a separate ticket window.

No.10 G.H.Wood on the centre road also joined in the party. A presentation was made to Mr Lambden, General Manager at the time. The locomotives in the rear of the picture above are No.14 Thornhill, originally built for the Manx Northern Railway, and No.3 Pender, among the line up of redundant locomotives on the old Peel departure road.

THE ISLE OF MAN RAILWAY

Short line working 1976

1975 and 1976 saw what was almost the end of the railway. Tynwald, the Manx parliament, had recommended that no further financial support should be given. The politicians had lost interest in the railway.

Douglas station was firmly locked shut, with rusting rails and total inactivity for two whole summer seasons. The 1975 season saw trains running only between Castletown and Port Erin, though the line opened back as far as Ballasalla in 1976.

Due to the fact that such a large proportion of visitors to the island lodged in Douglas, and travelling on the shortened railway involved a not-so-comfortable bus journey from Douglas to Ballasalla, it is not surprising that there was little interest in travelling on the train.

Hardly surprisingly, the short line operation was not a success, but fortunately the story since has been more hopeful. The political view of the future of the island's tourist industry changed, with the railway being seen as an important part of that industry.

Train services began operating again from Douglas in 1977 with Tynwald taking control.

Left: at Castletown the driver of No.4 Loch *attends to oiling the crosshead and slide bars.*

Below left: Loch *is watered and oiled ready for the return to Port Erin.*

Below: the crew return to the footplate ready for departure.

Right: an idyllic setting for a portrait.

Chapter 3

On shed at Douglas in the 1970s

Above: No.10 G.H.Wood *and No.4* Loch *coming off shed early one morning. Notice at this time that Douglas station was still complete with the two sets of platforms, canopies, and sidings. Many of the coaches also in this view originate from 1873, but almost all now have sadly been scrapped.*

Left: while most holidaymakers were still in their guest houses or hotels enjoying that second pot of tea at the breakfast table, some of the best railway action of the day was going on around Douglas engine shed. Here we see No.11 Maitland, *named after one of the early directors of the IoMR, creeping around Douglas yard preparing for the first duty of the day.*

Above: three for the price of one, a scene I have not witnessed again since this picture was taken. Three locos coupled together, and all in the same ('Ailsa' green) livery. It is also a reminder of the days of the old IoMR when the trains were put away at night! No.12 Hutchinson is in charge of No.4 Loch and No.10 G.H.Wood.

Right: this Wickham railcar was owned by the IoM Harbour Board and was formerly used on the Ramsey Pier tramway. It found its way onto the IoMR during the 1970s to assist with clearing the closed lines and the re-opening of the Douglas - Ballasalla section of the south line in 1976/7. The IoMR eventually cut it up, having broken it first!

Left: No.13 Kissack in 1973, running out of the shed yard to join its train. I can quite clearly remember walking onto Douglas station in the 1970s and thinking: "Not Kissack again!" In fact, No.13 was one of just a few stalwart locos that kept the railway running in the lean years of the 1970s.

Built in 1910, the engine was named after Edward Thomas Kissack, a Manxman and a director of the Isle of Man Railway. Withdrawn in 1991 for overhaul, it was decided to place its repaired boiler on No.10 G.H.Wood, just to see a different engine running. Kissack remained in pieces for a number of years but was restored to service in 2005.

It has always amazed me just how the brass numerals fit on and around the chimney, especially the thinner chimneys and the double figures! Try replicating it in 4mm scale and you will see what I mean.

Above: No.4 Loch *outside the running shed. There is an interesting collection of scrap to the left of the locomotive including an ancient railway delivery vehicle, of which at one time there were many. I believe this was JMN 538, a Morris Commercial 45/55cwt platform bodied lorry. A concrete coaling platform now takes up this area.* Loch *during this period had quite an assortment of tank patches that made it recognisable without the name or number.*

Below: No.10 G.H.Wood *inside the running shed at Douglas. The rear of former County Donegal railcar No.19 and an unidentified loco can also be seen. Note the 'shrubbery' on the walls and the clutter left around the shed: today's Health and Safety regulations ensure this is a clearer, brighter area, with whitewashed walls. Observe the dent in the rear cab sheet of* G.H.Wood *- many photographs exist of locos with similar dents in the same position. For years I could not find an explanation as to how they appeared, until a recent visit to the Douglas workshops when I was advised that they occur when the Douglas fitting shops hoist lifts the loco at the bunker end. This apparently always bashes and dents the cab sheet.*

Above: No.12 Hutchinson *pushes a cold No.4* Loch *into the running shed for attention. This photo highlights the different pattern of tank patches on each loco. In the 1980s/1990s most serviceable locomotives were to receive welded steel side tanks, and the lack of rivets unfortunately took away a lot of the original character - until simulated 'glue on' rivet heads were used!*

This 1973 scene gives such a different picture to the view from the end of the one existing platform today. The running shed building itself is no different, other than the colour the doors are painted, and gone is the body of Cleminson coach N41 which was used as a mess for so many years.

Above and above right: No.10 G.H.Wood *of 1905 in the running shed. No.10 spent longer periods in the sheds than most, or so it seemed on my visits to the island. It is seen here in front of an unidentified M wagon.*

Right: No.4 Loch *of 1874 waits patiently for its next duty at the back of the running shed. At one time* Loch *was one of the oldest operating locomotives in the world, a record only broken in recent years when No.1* Sutherland *of 1873 was restored in 1998. The nameplates on* Loch *and* Mona *had a slightly different style to the others in the fleet: the letters were split because the injector overflow pipes originally dissected them.*

On a bright sunny day the skylights in the roof of Douglas running shed gave a superb light for photography without the need for flash or fast film.

Chapter 4

Locomotive origins and details

The history of the Manx Beyer, Peacock locomotives has been well-documented in other publications and it should be well-known that no two are the same, as all have been partially or completely rebuilt during their lives, with the exception of No.16 *Mannin*, which has had the same external appearance throughout its working career. Engines have had pipes changed, re-routed or added, whistles swapped for different sizes and tones, differing types of safety valves, various sizes and shapes of chimneys, increased capacity side tanks, all with patches added in later years, handrails, cabs and cab spectacles altered, lamp brackets in various positions, and the inevitable boiler changes with increased capacities, etc.

From the outset, boilers were certainly exchanged between engines as well as new ones being ordered. Some locomotives became donors to keep the rest of the fleet running: for example, No.2 *Derby* was withdrawn in 1949 after boiler failure, and by 1951 the whole engine had become a source of spare parts. The practice of parts donation became particularly regular in the late 1950s, 1960s, and 1970s during the run-down and lack of expenditure on the railway. This gives each and every one of the sixteen engines their own personality despite the apparent standardisation.

Locomotive liveries have also gone through many changes and these range from dark green to the pre-Second World War Indian red and 'Ailsa' green. Varied historic liveries were to be seen on locos during the 1980s and 1990s through to the current Indian red from 2001. But the modeller should also be aware of differences in the liveries and the applications of that livery.

As an example, take the Indian red livery: in the original pre-war version that the footsteps to the cab are all black, whereas the current livery has the faces lined out in red and yellow.

Also note that prior to the use of the 'Ailsa' apple green livery in 1967, paint pigments were mixed by hand in the paint shop by the staff and differences in shade from one engine to another were quite common. Varnishing would also have had an effect on the finished colour, as would the many years of use, heat, and weathering. Changes in colour due to the ageing of original photographs, and the inaccuracies of most printed reproductions, can also be misleading.

For all these reasons, no two photographs of any particular IoMR locomotive seem to look identical, but they can provide valuable clues if you are modelling a specific loco at a certain period. Details like builders' plates were removed and replaced over time, chimney numerals disappeared and re-appeared, and there were many small variations in the position of the lining.

An odd example of detail is that, around 1968/9 when No.15 *Caledonia* was repainted from the short-lived 1967 reopening day 'Ailsa' green and reverted to Manx Northern Railway red, 'MNR No.4' was signwritten onto the tank sides, but the loco still carried the IoMR '15' in brass numerals on the chimney.

The origins of the Manx loco names have always been a source of fascination to me. Some of the history behind the locomotive names and the personalities involved has been documented, and in the course of research I have found more information about some of the worthies that have their names embellished onto the Manx engines.

Above and below: No.11 Maitland, *Beyer, Peacock works no.4663 of 1905. Detail differences can clearly be seen in these three views - those above and below were taken outside Douglas shed, that below right some years later at Port Erin shed. Many features can be picked out - the mechanical lubricator, the brass safety valve casing, the welded rivet-less tanks, pipe work, oil cans, and lining all show up well. It is also possible to distinguish between the liveries, even in black & white: in the earlier views the loco was painted bright orange-red and had no company crest; the later view shows the crest present and the machine back in the pre-war Indian red. Note that the style of the rear number has varied. The steam and oil weathering also shows up well.*

Locomotives of the Isle of Man railways

No./Name	Built	Works No.	Origins of name/notes	Condition/location (as at September 2007)
1 Sutherland	1873	BP 1253	Chairman of IoMR, cost £1,600	withdrawn 2002, dismantled, parts in Douglas running shed.
2 Derby	1873	BP 1254	Lord of Man, cost £1,600	dismantled and scrapped in 1951.
3 Pender	1873	BP 1255	Deputy Chairman, cost £1,600	withdrawn 1959. Currently in the Museum of Science & Industry, Manchester.
4 Loch	1874	BP 1416	former Governor	**in service.**
5 Mona	1874	BP 1417	ancient name for the island	withdrawn 1968. In store at back of Douglas carriage shed in very poor condition.
6 Peveril	1875	BP 1524	from the book 'Peveril of the Peak'	withdrawn 1960. Cosmetically restored 1997, Port Erin museum.
7 Tynwald	1880	BP 2038	Viking name of Manx Parliament	withdrawn 1939, dismantled 1945. Frames are still extant.
8 Fenella	1894	BP 3610	from the book 'Peveril of the Peak'	**in service.**
9 Douglas	1896	BP 3815	capital of the island	withdrawn 1953. In store at Douglas shed, unlikely to run again.
10 G.H.Wood	1905	BP 4662	Director of IoMR, cost £1,405	withdrawn pending fitting of new boiler (in hand).
11 Maitland	1905	BP 4663	Director of IoMR, cost £1,405	withdrawn pending fitting of new boiler (in hand).
12 Hutchinson	1908	BP 5186	Director of IoMR	**in service.**
13 Kissack	1910	BP 5382	Director of IoMR	**in service.**
14 Thornhill	1880	BP 2028	home of MNR Chairman, MNR No.3.	withdrawn 1963. Privately preserved on the island.
15 Caledonia	1885	Dübs 2178	Latin for Scotland, MNR No.4	**in service.**
16 Mannin	1926	BP 6296	Celtic for the island, cost £2,840	withdrawn 1964. Cosmetically restored 1997. On display in Port Erin museum.
17 Viking	1958	Schöma 2066	historical association, purchased 1992	**in service.**
18 Ailsa	1994	LD9342	after Lord Ailsa, built by Hunslet and acquired July 2005 from IRIS contractor.	**in service.**
19/20	1950/1	Walkers	bogie diesel railcars with power units by Walker Bros. of Wigan, purchased in1961 from the County Donegal Railways . Currently withdrawn, restoration pending.	

All steam locomotives with the exception of the Dübs 0-6-0T *Caledonia* are 2-4-0T, built by Beyer, Peacock, Gorton Foundry, Manchester. (BP)

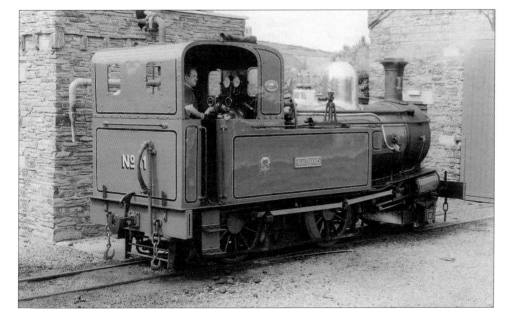

During the IoMR Company days, locomotives always ran chimney first out of Douglas, with exceptions for short periods. Engines No.1 *Sutherland*, No.7 *Tynwald* and No.14 *Thornhill* were turned at St.Johns in the mid-1920s. In more recent years, for special occasions, No.4 *Loch* and No.15 *Caledonia* have also been turned.

As far back as 1944 consideration was given either to acquiring diesel locomotives or converting steam locos to oil firing. Nothing was done regarding the oil firing, and it was not until 1992 that a diesel appeared on the Isle of Man Railway, in the shape of a Schöma industrial machine which became No.17 *Viking*.

However, two diesel railcars (Nos.19 & 20) were purchased from the closed County Donegal Railways in an attempt to reduce running expenses even further in the early 1960s; they were eventually put to use for many years as permanent way department transport.

New century, old liveries

Left: No.10 G.H.Wood *at Port Erin in 2001, giving a spirited performance on its departure for Douglas. Take note of the rear handrail, which varies in style and fixing on some locos.*

Below: No.10 G.H.Wood *seen at Port Erin in 2001, resplendent in the revised Indian red livery. This 1905-built locomotive has had a bumpy career, having been involved in several accidents, two of which caused severe damage to the chassis and almost put the engine beyond repair. In 1993 it was given the overhauled boiler and a number of other parts from No.13* Kissack. *The modern welded tanks have had stick-on rivets added - these give such a lot of character back to the locos, which looked very bland in the 1980s and 1990s. All that is missing are the tank patches!*

These railcars are now of historical interest themselves. Latterly they were showing signs of a lack of care and attention. They have been dismantled for restoration, but the decay found means that the project, whenever it may be finished, will result in replicas rather than restored units.

Certain locomotives have spent years idle, either on display at St.John's or Douglas stations, in the museum at Port Erin, or, as in the case of No.5 *Mona*, languishing at the back of the old carriage shed in Douglas for almost thirty years. It was moved out when that building was demolished, just long enough to be photographed in the Douglas running shed, then subsequently went into hiding once more.

Restorations which once would have been considered impossible have taken place successfully. No.15 *Caledonia* was the first and is in use today. No.1 *Sutherland* was also returned to traffic for a short while; however, after four years of active service, it is now unfortunately destined to be returned to the museum, hav-

ing given back the boiler borrowed from No.8 *Fenella*.

However, that is what the IoMR has always done, and shows the benefit of a 'standardised' loco fleet.

The Manx 2-4-0T locomotive design of 1873 can be traced back to many very similar Gorton engines. The design was produced in collaboration with Thomas Hunt of Crewe works. It had inclined outside cylinders, a sloping front to the smokebox (which was originally held together with bolts and not rivets!), and the Bissel patent pony truck.

Forty-one 2-4-0 passenger engines with tenders had been supplied in 1862 to the Tudela & Bilbao Railway to an order placed by Vignoles. In the same year, the design was adapted to 3'6" gauge for railways in Norway, with side tanks instead of a tender and a half wrap cab front sheet, very similar to the style carried by No.1 *Sutherland* on opening day.

With a gauge of 3', the first IoMR locomotives built in 1873 were the narrowest gauge engines built at Gorton to date. They cost the

newly-formed IoMR £4,800, or £1,600 each. In contrast, 53 years later in 1926 No.16 *Mannin* cost the IoMR £2,840. It was to be the last of its type built for any railway and the last narrow gauge locomotive built at the Gorton Foundry for use in the British Isles.

In 1945 Beyer, Peacock were asked to provide a design and cost for a 2-6-2 tank. Although the design went to a second revision, the price quoted was a prohibitive £12,250 each, and no order was placed.

A proposal to convert some of the 2-4-0T's to 2-4-2T to increase fuel and water capacity also came to nothing.

In 1939 No.7 *Tynwald* suffered severe damage in a collision with No.10 *G.H.Wood* in Oakhill cutting and by 1945 it had been dismantled and has remained so ever since. Whether this is due to the accident or other defects is not recorded. However, the engine has never officially been scrapped and the frames are still extant.

1949 saw the demise of another loco, No.2 *Derby*, with a weak boiler. The loco was dismantled in the early 1950s and scrapped shortly after. Parts were retained for use on the surviving fleet.

Sharp, Stewart and Co. of Atlas Works, Oxford Street, Manchester, was the second supplier of steam locomotives for the two main railway companies on the Isle of Man.

From the designs and specifications of W.H.Thomas, resident engineer of the Manx Northern Railway, the 'Sharpies', as they became affectionately known, were built and supplied in 1897 as the Manx Northern's first two engines.

| No.1 | *Ramsey* | works no.2855 |
| No.2 | *Northern* | works no.2856 |

Costing £1,100 each they were to a similar specification as the Isle of Man Railway's Beyer, Peacock engines, but looking quite different with straight footplate, larger water tanks, and a radial front axle behind the cylinders instead of the pony truck ahead of them.

These engines were purchased on the grounds of lower cost, and they lacked the refinement of the Beyer, Peacock machines.

It is interesting to note that the Manx Northern's third locomotive was a Beyer,Peacock product, matching the IoMR engines. No.3 *Thornhill* later became No.14 in the IoMR fleet.

Following amalgamation of the IoMR and the MNR in 1905, the two 'Sharpies' had a chequered career, and after the IoMR took delivery of No.12 *Hutchinson* in 1908 and No.13 *Kissack* in 1910, the two non-standard Manx Northern engines became surplus to requirements and were subsequently condemned by the IoMR management.

Ramsey was little used, except for permanent way work and on the harbour tramway in Ramsey, which was at this time considered unsuitable for the Beyer,Peacock engines. Otherwise, it sat in Ramsey shed until 1923 when it was dismantled.

Northern was sold for the sum of £78 in 1912, taken to Douglas, and cut up.

Above: No.12 Hutchinson *leaving Castletown in August 2001. Note the addition of raised platforms. The only through stations that had these previously were Port Soderick, Port St.Mary, Sulby Glen, Peel Road, Union Mills, and St.John's.*

Below left: No.6 Peveril *had been cosmetically restored by the Isle of Man Steam Railway Supporters Association a few years earlier in the Indian red. It is seen inside the Douglas running shed in 2000.*

Below: outside Port Erin shed driver Jeff Kelly gives No.12 Hutchinson *the once-over with the oil cans in August 2001.*

Left: No.4 Loch at Douglas in May 2003. The engine had been out of use for some years, having been withdrawn from service during the winter of 1996, subsequently being stored in Douglas engine shed and then displayed in the museum at Port Erin. Loch seems to have become one of the most popular engines on the railway and the Supporters' Association were not going to let her 'rest in peace'! Under the slogan "Un-Loch your cash" a fund was started in 1998 to help restore the loco. She was handed back to the IoMR, and returned to service on 8th August 2002 in the current Indian red livery but retaining the Manx Northern Railway style 'three legs' and numeral on the front buffer beam (the only engine in the current IoMR fleet to carry such details), the older style steam dome, and the original large Beyer, Peacock builder's plate (below) on the cab side sheet.

Below: two views taken in Douglas engine shed on 19th May 2003. No.8 Fenella last steamed in 1969 on the Port Erin line, having spent most of its life working on the Peel and Ramsey routes. It was put into storage for some ten years until the Isle of Man Railway Preservation Society purchased the loco along with No.5 Mona and No.9 Douglas. It has, like all the locos in the fleet, undergone many boiler changes during its life. A special 2'10¾" diameter boiler was fitted in 1935/6 and it was during this boiler change that Fenella lost its sloping smokebox front, which was retained by the other smaller engines.

Regaining its boiler from No.1, the locomotive was being rebuilt to its original condition. The sloping smokebox complete with the chimney and 385 gallon side tanks from No.1 Sutherland had already been fitted - the latter complete with nameplates intact. No.8's chimney sits on the side awaiting fitting. Fenella was returned to traffic on the 5th September 2003 after some 35 years of being without steam.

When Fenella's boiler was removed from No.1 Sutherland it was discovered that Sutherland was in a very poor condition. Despite its historical interest, it may be some years before it is running again.

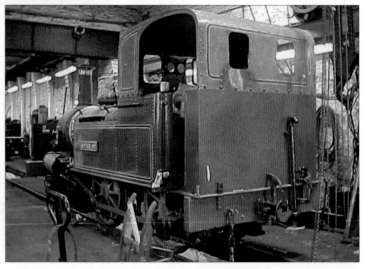

Above: No.11 Maitland has been in a red livery for some years as seen in this 1998 view at Port Erin. The loco looks quite different from the 1970s pictures - welded side tanks, tapered chimney with numerals, the polished brass safety valve casing (peculiar to this loco) returned, and the twin Ross 'pop' valves moved well forward of their normal position on the boiler.

Right: the 2001 season saw the demise of the different 'historical' liveries and the return of the post-war Indian red to the entire fleet of locomotives, with red and cream coaches. No.16 Mannin was repainted during the refurbishment of the Port Erin museum in 1997. In the course of this cosmetic restoration it was discovered that part of the coal bunker was made of plywood!

The odd man out

Caledonia, colloquially known as 'The Cale', was the 'odd man out'. It was the only 0-6-0 and the only Dübs locomotive on the island.

Built as No.4 for the Manx Northern Railway in 1885, it was ideal for the heavy mineral trains on the 1 in 49 gradients of the Foxdale Railway.

After 1905 it was little used except for snow clearance duties in IoMR days. It was alleged that it spread the gauge and was too heavy, and it has been suggested that its lack of use was because the crews did not like working on the engine as it was apparently difficult to steam.

It appeared in many liveries - MNR red (as in these pictures), MNR simplified red, IoMR dark green and by 1964, IoMR unlined Indian red. In 1967 it was painted 'Ailsa' green for a very short period and by 1969 it was in a lookalike MNR red. At the time of writing, it carries North Eastern Railway dark blue - complete with rust and dirt!

Withdrawn in 1968, *Caledonia* was eventually put on display in the museum at Port Erin where she spent some twenty years. In 1993 it was taken back to Douglas for inspection with a view to possible restoration. These pictures show the result.

As MNR No.4, *Caledonia* returned in summer 1995 to the Snaefell Mountain Railway, where it had been used some hundred years before on the construction of that line. (A third rail was laid to 3' gauge on part of the route for the purpose.)

Above: 'No.4' Caledonia *stands outside Douglas running shed in 1995 resplendent in the replica 'Manx Northern' red livery.*

Below: ash being removed from the smokebox in 1998. The locomotive to the right is the then newly restored No.1 Sutherland.

Above: off territory - from 2,036' above sea level on Snaefell, No.15 Caledonia, Manx Electric Railway trailer No.57, and a Snaefell Mountain Railway motor car to aid braking, descend as a lone SMR car ascends the western side of the mountain. Having been enclosed within the Port Erin museum and Douglas shed for so many years, Caledonia was restored especially for the centenary of the 3'6" gauge Snaefell Mountain Railway in 1995. A third rail was temporarily laid to 3' gauge between Bungalow and the summit to enable the steam loco to run in commemoration of its work during the original construction of the line.

It is said that on clear day you can see six king-doms from the summit of Snaefell: Scotland, Ireland, Wales, England, Mann - and Heaven.

Mann (Celtic), or currently Man, is a separate kingdom and not part of the United Kingdom. The present Queen is known on the island as the 'Lord of Man'. This title was formerly held by the Stanley family, the Earls of Derby.

Above: No.15 Caledonia at Port Erin in 1995, in the livery of her former owners, the Manx Northern Railway.

Right: in 2001 Caledonia had its five year over-haul. The boiler was sent to England, the rest of the engine being dealt with in Douglas. The loco is seen here standing outside the workshops shortly after steam tests following re-assembly. I had hoped to see this locomotive painted in the 'Ailsa' green livery, which it carried for a short time in 1968. Our first visit to the loco shed in Douglas in 2001 found the loco being made ready for one of its first steamings since overhaul. My daughter asked the fireman on board why it had been paint-ed blue. "What the boss says, goes!" and the boss wanted blue, apparently from a liking for the Great Eastern Railway livery. I must admit it looks won-derful - the superbly exquisite lettering and lining is straight from the Victorian era in which the loco was built.

Chapter 5

Traces of the closed lines

A selection of historic images and a selective tour of the visible remnants of the civil engineering and architecture of the closed lines - west to Peel, the Foxdale branch, and north to Ramsey.

Over a number of visits to the island during the 1970s, 1980s, and 1990s, I took photographs of the remaining infrastructure of the closed lines to observe details of the architecture, lineside features, and environment. As it turned out, some of the early 1970s views were taken just in time: returning to some of the sites in more recent years, many items had been dismantled or removed for ever.

West to Peel

Visits to St.John's in the early years after closure, 1973/4, saw the whole site still resembling a railway station. It was complete with track, station nameboards, signal box, grounded four-wheel coach bodies, water towers, and the ornate Norwegian-style station building.

The corrugated iron carriage shed still had a full complement of coaching stock, although very vandalised, and such a waste of the island's railway heritage. The stories about this site during removal of the railway infrastructure years later are not worth repeating here.

These closed lines still hold interest for many enthusiasts, even after some thirty years. Those which have been converted into footpaths are most definitely worth the effort to walk, not just for the research but the views of wonderful Manx countryside and coastline.

The Peel to Douglas line has been converted into a footpath, which can be walked or cycled from Union Mills to Peel. The section between Quarter Bridge and Braddan now forms part of the TT races relief road.

The concrete platforms and road overbridges are still *in situ* at Kirk Braddan and Union Mills, and certain crossing gate lodges can be found further down the track, but you will be hard pressed to find any trace of the station at Crosby which has been completely obliterated. A very overgrown Foxdale line overbridge at St.John's is still just visible and the only part of the original IoMR St.John's station that can still be seen.

Peel still boasts a station building and goods shed which have been incorporated now into the 'House of Manannan' museum. The brick and slate water tower still stands near the site of the level crossing.

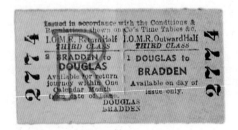

Above: Braddan station in August 1955. This picture illustrates just what an operation the Sunday special services from Douglas to Braddan were. These specials would normally bring passengers to Braddan and then travel on to Union Mills empty, run round there, and return to await the end of the church service.

Here we see the crowds returning to the station with No.5 Mona and eight coaches standing in the station with the first of what appears to be three trains in view, involving perhaps some twenty-five coaches and three locos, such was the popularity of the services.
Photo: the late David Odabashian.

Below: At Braddan, the first station on the Peel line, the building was no more than a wooden shed with a corrugated iron roof. It is seen here well after closure and removal of the rails, in a faded and peeling final paint finish of maroon and cream. All the Peel line stations were of wood, with the exception of Peel itself (though the original build-

ing there was also wood), and spent most of their life painted in green or maroon and cream. This building was moved shortly after this photo was taken and rebuilt at Colby on the Port Erin line. In its present form the two front panels have been removed to make an open shelter.

Above: Crosby goods shed is a typical piece of narrow gauge architecture. It was kept out of sight of the travelling public for many years by a long advertising hoarding placed between the running line and the front of the shed, originally intended to disguise the manure siding. This was the only goods shed on the system built to this 'Norwegian' design. It must have been quite impractical for its intended use. In this 1950s view we can see just how much junk has accumulated and how badly stacked the parcels and packages are within the shed. Photo: the late David Odabashian.

Above: Union Mills. This was once one of the prettiest stations on the system, with superb gardens within which the name was spelled out in stones. Set unusually on a reverse curve, with a sweeping platform on the down side, Union Mills was no more than a Class Five station and so only a 'grand' style of hut was provided for a station building, but the site still managed to boast a stationmaster and a station clock at one time.

Right: Braaid Road, between Union Mills and Crosby. These outhouses were called crossing lodges, but were really no more than small stone huts.

Below: Crosby. The station buildings there and at St.John's are virtually identical, of 'Norwegian' character with red/pink zinc diamond roof tiles, cream diagonal wooden boarding, and green structural timbers, making them quite distinctive.

There was enough room in these small buildings for a general waiting room, ladies waiting room, and staff accommodation including a porter's room, station clerk, and booking office.

This style of station building never found its way onto the south line.

Above: St.John's - change for Peel, Ramsey, and Foxdale. Two railway companies originally operated through or from here, the Isle of Man Railway, Douglas to Peel, and the Manx Northern Railway, originally with a separate station for trains to Ramsey. The latter company also operated the Foxdale Railway until both were absorbed into the IoMR in 1905. The main station building was of the same 'Norwegian' style as Crosby - the only difference appears to have been the toilet facilities. At one time the station boasted a stone and timber footbridge, but it is unclear when this was removed. Most people would simply walk across the track. A sizeable three-road corrugated iron carriage shed was built behind the signal box in 1905. After the Peel and Ramsey lines were closed in 1968, a large collection of stock remained in store at this shed. I can still visualise the rows of bright red & cream coaches standing silent in the shed but, as can be seen by the leading coach in the photograph (left), they were all well vandalised. A series of fires also destroyed many items. The remaining contents of the shed subsequently went for scrap when the infrastructure was dismantled in 1974/5, thus much of the historic rolling stock heritage was lost. What a waste.

Below: just a few hundred yards north along the road towards the village is the original Manx Northern Railway terminus at St.John's. This brick building was erected in 1886. After closure of the branch, the station building was purchased around 1940 for use as a private dwelling. It is still occupied today, although very overgrown on the platform side. When this picture was taken it had the addition of a porch, otherwise it was in original condition, including paint colours. Architecturally it is almost identical to the building at Foxdale, except for some additional windows and a slight variation in chimney design.

Right: two lines left St.John's towards the west as if the railway had been built as double track. In fact they were two single lines, the line to Peel on the left and the Ramsey route to the right. They parted company about a mile further west of this point, with the Ramsey line taking a sharp rising right hand curve to the north crossing over the A1 Douglas to Peel road. The Peel line followed the course of the River Neb over which this girder bridge carries both lines, shortly after the level crossing at St.John's station. Note the two different types of track – the Peel rails are spiked whilst the Ramsey rails are chaired. This photo was taken looking west in 1954 well after the MNR ceased to exist; as it was known to have 'chaired' certain sections of track, it is possible that these were original MNR fittings.

The rakes of coaches on the far right are standing on the Foxdale branch tracks, towards St.John's West station
Photo: the late David Odabashian.

Above: the signal box at the eastern (Douglas) end of St.John's station. Apart from Douglas this was the only signal box on the island's railway system. Its stark interior was not the most homely of places, unlike some signal boxes. Constructed by the Manx Northern, it was a stone-built affair with wood boarding and glazing topped with a slate roof. It contained a ten lever frame. Not all train control was carried out from this box. An additional padlocked Stevens and Son ground frame was used for the Foxdale branch, and there were further ground levers at the Peel end for Peel trains.

Above: one of two water towers at St.John's, situated on the Douglas end of the island platform; a smaller tower was sited at the Ramsey end.

The grounded coach body originally on this platform was one of many 'Pairs' coach bodies dumped at the station when their underframes were used to create the runners for the 'Man-tainor' service in 1968.

Peel

Above the whole of Peel station as viewed in July 1956 from Peel Hill high above the River Neb and the city. The site was an elongated triangle and was by this date surrounded by roads on all three sides; some buildings were there before the railway in 1873 and still exist to this day. Many structures around the station were connected with the production of the famous Manx kippers.

At this time the engine shed still had the 1920s extension that was destroyed by fire - the date has not been recorded, but it was before the 1967 re-opening. The white building to the left of the station is a public house which pre-dated the railway but was renamed The Railway Hotel when the line opened; since the railway's closure it has been known as The Creek Inn.

It is worth noting that the River Neb is tidal and therefore can be modelled with the tide in or out, with water or just mud flats.

Photo: the late David Odabashian.

Above: Mill Road crossing gates, the water tower, and the engine shed. The 1907-built water tower has a slate tank built on a Peel sandstone base, much darker in colour than the engine shed, which was constructed in 1908. The posts just visible in front of the shed are the remains of a corrugated iron extension.

Right: Peel station, from the railway boundary fence on Harbour Road. An excellent collection of 1960s/1970s road vehicles, the most modern being the Commer van and the Austin Mini.

THE ISLE OF MAN RAILWAY

Left: Peel station from the roadside. The original station building was of wooden construction, and in a slightly different position. The structure seen here was built in 1907/8 in mock-Tudor style with pink stucco walls topped with red terracotta tiles. The goods shed was of similar construction. This building and the goods shed now form part of the House of Manannan museum.

The Foxdale Branch

The line clung to the mountainside for some two and a half miles up a 1 in 49 gradient all the way from St.John's. It had mixed fortunes, being opened in 1886 for the mines traffic which proved to be short-lived, and was closed around 1940, but the track was still *in situ* until 1975.

The line can still be walked almost for its entire length, except for a small area around the Foxdale River and the embankment at St.John's.

The views down the valley are stunning.

It must have been quite a sight early in the line's history watching *Caledonia* (or any other locomotive, come to that) travelling up and down the valley on this gradient, with heavy trainloads of coal up and mine products and waste down.

Many railway artefacts can still be found on the Foxdale branch. There are even telegraph poles still in evidence. Foxdale station still exists, as do a number of concrete overbridges, quite different to those found elsewhere on the system. The concrete and stone viaduct over the Foxdale River at St.John's still stands, except for the two plate girders.

In 1926, while the station was still open to railway traffic, the building was converted into a house, occupied by the line's guard.

Above: the Foxdale River bridge at St.John's. In technical terms this is a viaduct. At some 37' above the river level, it consisted of two 47'6' steel plate girders placed on a 5' wide concrete and stone central pier to take the Foxdale Railway across the Castletown Road and Foxdale River at St.John's.

Below: the station building at the terminus of the Foxdale line, seen here in its later role as a schoolhouse. It was built of red brick with quoins and several string courses of yellow stone, under a grey slate roof. The frontage on the platform side had a recessed sheltered porch with a wood and glass screen.

North to Ramsey

The line north to Ramsey is walkable in sections from St.Germains as far as the Wildlife Park north of Ballaugh. Peel Road is now just a memory although the Peel Road overbridge still stands unfilled, whilst St.Germains has been converted into a very pleasant looking dwelling.

The builders of the Manx Northern Railway line encountered a number of large-scale civil engineering projects in completing the link to Ramsey. Most of them can still be seen, in part if not completely.

Devil's Elbow, known locally as 'Gob-y-Deigan', troublesome for the entire history of the railway, is remembered for the numerous landslips.

There was a lattice iron viaduct across Glen Mooar, with three 60' spans and a 75' drop to the bottom of the glen, while Glen Wyllin viaduct was a little lower, just 60' high and with solid plate girders - by narrow gauge standards very impressive. Both viaducts were supported on two red Peel sandstone central piers, with similar stone buttresses to the embankments. By the time I photographed these viaducts, only the stonework was still intact. It still is, but trees in the Glen Mooar valley block the view, and some are now even taller than the 75' piers.

Kirk Michael station and goods shed has a new use as a fire station complete with a complementary crossing gate!

Sulby Glen has also been turned into a private house.

Ramsey has been wiped away by a bakery and an industrial estate.

Above: Ballaleece overbridge. This plate girder bridge takes the Ramsey line over the St.John's to Peel Road. The bridge was located shortly after the Peel and Ramsey lines diverged.

Below: St.Germains, the first proper station on this route, in August 1955, seen from the north.

Below left: St.Germains station building, in the style very typical of the Manx Northern Railway, an almost standardised design, the first proper station on this route. It was built substantially of red Peel sandstone, double gabled with tall chimneys. It is in a very bleak lonely location, and was built so the MNR could serve Peel. When Peel Road station was opened, St.Germains was closed for a short period c.1889/1890 and the original loop and siding were lifted. The station was restored following public pressure, although the loop was not replaced until 1928 and the siding a year later.

Both photos: the late David Odabashian.

Above: a Manx Northern Railway lineside gate, on a farm crossing near Gob-ny-Creggan, just south of Glen Mooar. There were many of these such gates all using locally found unfinished Manx grey slate posts and wrought iron gates.

Below: as well as the large bridges and surviving stonework, the footpath from St.Germains still reveals much about its railway origins. Although carrying a replacement galvanised farm gate, the two darker square gateposts are of Manx Northern Railway origin, made of cast iron with a single 45° support to each. There are many varieties of fence posts and other artefacts still to be found along this path.

Above: Ballakaighen footbridge. Set in Ballakaighen cutting 4½ miles north of St.John's, this fine footbridge of MNR origin was of simple construction, on masonry pillars with timber decking. It was photographed in 1998 whilst walking the north line trackbed, which was very boggy and wet here, and I can see how the railway had so much trouble with landslides at Donkey Bank (Gob-y-Deigan). The bridge was apparently already in a bad state in the 1960s, but some thirty years later it still stands, though just about everything is now out of true, bent, or leaning, but it retains a wonderful character.

Right a view of Ballaquine skew bridge taken in 1999 - it is remarkable that so little change is evident, apart from the track being lifted. There is certainly little sign of decay or overgrown plant life. The bridge is situated just north of the Donkey Bank, Gob-y-Deigan, between St.Germains and Glen Mooar, and was built to carry the A4 Peel - Kirk Michael road over the railway. In 2001 road signs advised that the bridge was weak and no doubt the Highways Board will not maintain it indefinitely. The trackbed is now a footpath between St.Germains and Glen Mooar.

Considerable amounts of Peel red sandstone and Manx slate form the abutments and side walls, and some 100' of structure and considerable steelwork was needed to cross a road just 30' wide.

Top: St.Germains station building in use as a private dwelling in the 1970s, with track removed - but no less remote.

Above: Glen Mooar viaduct in 1954 - an interesting view as one can see the whole of the 75' high piers and the bridge over the stream that follows the valley floor down to the beach. The growth of trees and other flora makes this view impossible now. Each of the three steel lattice girders was 60' long. Glen Mooar viaduct was one of two major civil engineering features on the Ramsey line, the other being a similar structure a few miles north at Glen Wyllin.
Photo: the late David Odabashian.

Above: the remains of the viaduct looking west, seaward from the glen. Taken in the 1980s this view is now impossible as the trees have grown up. To the right and below the foliage is the stream that starts at the top of the Glen at a waterfall called the White Spout (Spooyt Vane). A grassy path runs the length of the glen.

Right: the surviving abutments and piers in 1975, seen from the southern slope of the glen west of the viaduct. Although the lattice girders are long gone, the stonework proved remarkably resilient.

Right: by the time this photos was taken (1975), the three girders that spanned this deep glen some 75' below had been removed. This is the original stonework from 1879, and is a mixture of Peel sandstone, Manx slate, and concrete. These piers have withstood 120 years or so quite well, especially considering how close they are to the sea and subject to the prevailing Irish Sea winds. The metalwork was not so hard wearing, however - the original MNR spans were life expired by around 1920, so replacement was carried out here and at Glen Wyllin by the IoMR before 1921. It was an elaborate project using a number of cranes, lifting legs attached to the stonework, and several locomotives each side of the ravine.

Below: looking seaward (west) from the southern embankment with the top of the first abutment just visible. This embankment is extremely steep compared to the northern side. Just below the tree line is the entrance to the Glen, the narrow A4 road from Peel to Kirk Michael, and a number of small dwellings leading to the beach.

Below right: from the southern end of the viaduct we look east over the entire glen. Note how steep the sides of this valley are throughout. Beyond the glen are the mountains of Sartfell, Slieau Freoaghane, and Slieau Dhoo.

Left: beneath the northern span of Glen Mooar ran a fairly fast flowing stream, which eventually reached the sea a few hundred yards away. At the foot of the pier is this stone bridge over the stream, leading from the path in the glen to the pier for no apparent reason.

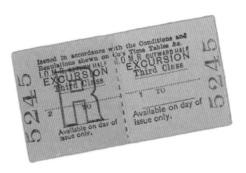

Above: a few miles further north, almost into Kirk Michael, is Glen Wyllin viaduct, similar in appearance to that at Glen Mooar. The steelwork here was plate girders, with spans of the same length but at 60' not as far above the glen.

Glen Wyllin is now a campsite, very popular with locals and visitors to the island alike, and very different to the days when one could go motor boating, play on the amusements, play bowls, and dine in the restaurant in what was then a railway-owned park. Picturesque, enclosed by some superb trees and woodland, it still holds the memory of the railway with the viaduct piers still in situ.

Taken in 2001, the photographs show the north end stone abutment and pad on which the girder would have rested. Considering the time lapse, the steel on all the piers appears well preserved.

The steep path and steps led up the embankment and along the side of the track to Kirk Michael station.

Below: Kirk Michael on 29th May 1953, showing the goods shed, station building, and level crossing, looking south towards St.John's.
Photo: the late David Odabashian.

Right: Kirk Michael looking north.

Below: photographed from the level crossing gates, the permanent way heading south here appears to run away to infinity, but gives a very deceptive view of the landscape. With the Kirk Michael home signal just visible, this short wide cutting ends abruptly about 150 yards from here and drops some 65' into Glen Wyllin. The railway crosses the glen on the three span plate girder viaduct. The unpainted picket fence to the left protects the footpath to the railway-owned Glen Wyllin amusement park. I well remember walking this path at the tender age of eight with my parents and picking bluebells after the day's visit to the park.
Photo: the late David Odabashian.

Below right: the water tower at Kirk Michael was situated the other side of the road crossing gates. The loco on a southbound train had to draw across the level crossing without the coaches in order to obtain water without blocking the road. Northbound services stopped to water before dropping passengers at the station.

Left: Kirk Michael. I have fond memories of this station from 1964 - it was the furthest north I can remember travelling on the IoMR, for a day trip to the railway-owned facilities at Glen Wyllin. There was a path, protected from the railway by an unpainted picket fence, which followed the line for about half a mile back down towards the Glen Wyllin viaduct, and then dropped steeply down the embankment into the glen.

This station is of the standard Manx Northern style, like St.Germains, double gabled, of red sandstone with a grey slate roof. The station boasted quite a large goods shed.

Although seen here very closed, the track has not been lifted in places, and the whole scene looks as if it could be waiting for the next train.

The two buildings today serve as a fire station. A small piece of track and a crossing gate have been put back as a reminder of its recognisable past as railway station, and you can still walk the path to and from Glen Wyllin.

Above: Glen Ballyre or Glion Balleira bridge. Most of the photos in this section were taken in the 1970s on a cycle ride from Douglas, around 35 miles! The bridge has some unusually shaped buttresses, which were added by the IoMR who apparently viewed the existing stonework with suspicion.

Right and below: Sulby Glen, probably the most picturesque station on the MNR, it was like no other on the railway system. On a raised platform, capable of holding three coach lengths, the station building had a distinctive roofed awning, taking up half the gable and roof of grey slate, the other half covering the station itself.

The coping stones on the slopes at each end of the platforms had to be inset so as not to foul the running boards of the coaches.

The only other buildings or facilities at this station were a short goods siding and small wooden shed, but these had all been cleared away by the time these photos were taken. There was no run round or passing loop.

Right and below: Sulby Bridge - another typical MNR station, or lodge, as they have been described. Although it was nearer to the village of Sulby than was Sulby Glen, most villagers and visitors alike apparently used the latter station. These standardised station buildings were large enough to contain a spacious waiting room and booking office on one side while on the other there was a lamp room and a ladies waiting room. The gentlemen's convenience was, of course, on the outside.

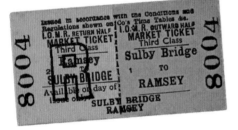

Below: Ramsey station, the headquarters of the Manx Northern, was in architectural terms quite different to all the other stations on its line, with some fine Italianate features and painted cement rendered walls. The building offered spacious accommodation, including a refreshment room. When this photo was taken only the station building remained on the site - the carriage and engine sheds, along with all the other structures, had gone. The station building made way for a bakery in 1978.

Chapter 6

Signalling and Permanent Way

Signals and related equipment are prominent characteristic elements and should be observed by careful modellers, while other trackside fittings, and even the track itself, also deserve attention.

Now we get right down to track level, literally.

This section is all about attention to detail, and a look at some of the infrastructure the railway passenger would not always notice - or probably even want to look at! The track and trackside features are what make the railway and its surrounding environment within the boundary of the line. Some things you really need to go looking for, others just appear and you think that it might be nice to reproduce them on a layout.

Trackwork on the IoMR has undergone quite a transformation in recent years: it is now more like a standard well-laid and bal-lasted railway throughout. In the past that was not the case. Track appeared to be lightly laid and frequently far from level. It was buried in weeds, grass, mud, or ash with all sorts of different textures. So it is no use laying model track with regular standard gauge ballast.

Curves were definitely far from smooth too, usually more of a succession of roughly bent rails laid like the sides of a 50 pence piece!

Above: round sleepers were used at first on the IoMR - rails were spiked to the sleepers, which were then buried to rail top level in whatever mineral was available for ballast. An example can be seen in the Museum at Port Erin.

The Manx Northern used conventional shaped sleepers from the start. The section near Gob-y-Deigan and some curves, along with the Foxdale line, had used chaired track.

Covering the sleepers and rails in ballast result-ed in corrosion so in later years ballasting was only to sleeper level, except within most station

Below: during 2000 a controversial decision was taken to lay a new pipeline from Meary Veg, south of Crogga Woods near Santon, towards Port Erin on the route of the railway trackbed. Many saw this as heralding the end of the railway, which now brings in valuable business for many Manx traders.

The work did limit operations to some short workings for a number of seasons, but a growing need for and interest in public transport both for local residents and visitors has resulted in the entire railway to Port Erin being relaid with new

boundaries where the track often seemed to be nothing more than two grooves in the mud.

There were periods when the main line track could not be seen for weeds, moss, and grass.

Ballast was taken from the pits at St.John's or other local sources. However, the Foxdale Railway and parts of the Manx Northern used the spoil waste from the mines at Foxdale. This spoil contained lead, and areas ballasted with it did not allow weeds to grow. The Foxdale line track which was still in place in the 1970s was virtually free of weeds even after 20 years or so out of use.

modern track. Gone are the staggered curves and track buried in mud, gravel, or ash with rails that were once spiked to the all-too-often rotten sleep-ers - along with a lot of the old IoMR charm and permanent way fixtures. Instead there are new sleepers, with Pandrol clips to retain the heavier rails (below), smoother turnouts, and consequent-ly the ability to run at higher speeds with a smoother, more comfortable ride. This will also presumably result in less wear and tear on the his-toric rolling stock.

A section on signals would not be complete without some reference to the signal box in Douglas. Dutton & Co. of Worcester installed this to replace the original basic signalling equipment of 1873.

From a visit to the box in the 1970s I remember a somewhat stark interior. A small stove, a wooden desk, one chair, and a smaller than normal track diagram above the levers.

The levers were coloured as follows:

Distant signals	green
Stop/Home signals	red
Point levers	black
Locking bars	blue
Spares (of which there were three)	white

The signals in Douglas, unlike most of the rest of the system, had twin spectacles with red and green lenses. There were also some specialised shunting signals and several grand gantry signals to protect the area.

Loco drivers used different whistle codes to inform the signalman as trains approached Douglas so the road could be set for the correct platform.

Right: the interior of Douglas signal box c.1958 with Bob Tate the duty signalman. Note the Dutton levers are upright with forward-facing handles when in the off position, with the handle upright when pulled on.
Photo: Tony Hill collection.

Below: the exterior of the signal box in May 1953. The corrugated iron clad structure behind is the carriage shed.
Photo: the late David Odabashian.

Left: the unloved signal box in the 1990s when the corrugated iron carriage shed behind still contained large amounts of railway history.

Above: a more recent (2000) view of the signal box at Douglas. The whole structure had been moved across the yard to stand next to the tracks once again and put back into proper use.

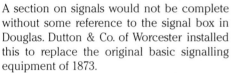

Above: No.4 Loch shunting a coach at Douglas station to strengthen a busy early morning train in 1974 - this was a common activity at one time; coaches were added as the need arose. The corrugated iron carriage shed, the signal box, and one of the wonderful bracket signals are all still in their rightful positions - before the buses and a supermarket invaded the site. As a young volunteer in 1973 I had the task of repainting these signals - great fun!

Below 1 & 2: front and back views of the up home at Port Soderick, just on the edge of Crogga Woods. Most IoMR signal posts away from the termini did not have ornate finials, just a simple sloping top. Note that these signals have only one spectacle frame, which would have contained a red lens. Green was not used for signalling in early IoMR days - the 'all clear' was white, so at night, if the line was clear, the train crew would see the white from the oil lamp on the signal post.

Below 3 & 4: one of the earliest IoMR signals still remains near Mill Road, Castletown - a slotted post signal, supplied by Linley & Co., of the type operated by the windlass from the station platforms. The iron pole on the side of the signal supported the lamp which turned, rather than an extra lens on the signal arm. This 1873 signal succumbed to old age in 2005 and today sits in Douglas workshops, its fate uncertain.

Opposite page 1: this signal was at Santon on the Port Erin line, but its origins are Manx Northern. The MNR home or starter signal arms originally had a V-shaped cutout at the end, similar to a normal distant signal, but in later years the V was cut off.

2. Photographed in 1970 in its original position, well after the line had closed and most of the Ramsey site had been erased, this was the Ramsey home signal - a typical MNR signal with conical cap and spike finial. The signal arm is an example of the 'fish tail' home, peculiar to the MNR. Also still in evidence is the single lens spectacle.

3. These former MNR signals protected the junctions opposite the signal box and within the confines of the station at St.John's. The top signal was for Peel services moving into the southern platform and the bottom signal was for Ramsey bound trains. Note the fine fretwork between the spectacle frames. Photo: the late David Odabashian.

4. Two types of Dutton signal arms from the gantry at the entrance to Douglas station. The type with the white bar is a home signal to allow trains into the station; the one with the white circle is described as being for 'Diverging Movements' - presumably to direct an arriving train to the right platform.

Above: No.4 Loch leaves Douglas with a late morning departure in 1974. To the left of the picture is the grand signal bracket that was once attached to the water tower and protected the entrance to Douglas station.

Right: despite having some 46 route miles, the IoMR only possessed one signal box outside Douglas, at the east (Douglas) end of St.John's station, seen here in June 1954. It was built in 1879 by the Manx Northern at the insistence of the IoMR purely for the protection of the IoMR Douglas - Peel line. It was at this point that the MNR had its only connection with the Peel railway. Although the MNR built the box and linked the ten lever frame with the points and signals for both routes, it was the IoMR who appointed a signalman to operate it. The signal box controlled all the train movements at the Douglas end of St.John's. The west end, including the Foxdale route, was controlled entirely by hand operated ground levers.

The ancient signal in the foreground is an 1873 IoMR slotted starter for Douglas-bound services which survived in use until the 1968 closure. The lamp operation is slightly different to the one illustrated at Mill Road on the Castletown line. The lamp was placed on the top of the post, and a crank was operated to remove the red glass disc and show the white light for the all clear. Photo: the late David Odabashian.

Top left: it was not just in the locomotive work-shops that the IoMR recycled items from other quarters. Many things from around the system were simply swapped or re-sited, and with the integration of all the island railways and tramways into 'Isle of Man Railways', this recycling continues on a wider scale.

This type of lever was to be found all around the Douglas station site, and examples can also be found today on the Manx Electric Railway.

Above and above right: two types of IoMR point lever; the type above was made by A.C.Nelson & Co. Many styles could be found over the system.

Below left: the Linley & Co. windlass, placed on station platforms or close by, was used to work home signals. They were fairly crude in their oper-ation. A chain was supplied to restrain the wheel whilst holding the signal in the 'all clear' position but if the chain went missing, anything to hand could be used, such as a shovel or block of wood. This example is at Castletown.

Right: there was rudimentary interlocking between points and signals. St.Germains, August 1955.

Below and below right: two examples of the Stevens & Son patent signal lever.

Many original IoMR details have sadly been removed forever and are now not there to photograph, or certainly not in their original position if they do still exist. Therefore, it is essential to look at examples in museums or consult archive material and publications.

For example, original IoMR gradient posts are now all gone, fences and fence posts have been modernised, and level crossing gates, such as at Ballasalla, are replacements.

Signalling has seen many historical types disappear, sometimes because modern systems with colour lights have been installed, especially at Douglas. However, signals of both IoMR and MNR origin can be found at various locations along the Port Erin line, some still very much in use. Odd signal arms and equipment are also exhibited in the museum at Port Erin and at the Narrow Gauge Museum at Tywyn in Wales.

Below: the IoMR was a typical narrow gauge line in as much as it does not seem to have had a standard type of stop block. No terminus or siding end was ever the same. Many were no more than sleepers dumped across the ends of the rails, though Douglas did have some fine timber baulk blocks. The most common form simply has posts of old rail with a timber cross beam, upon which is fixed centrally a metal plate to protect the wood from the hook of the centre chopper coupling. The example below was formerly at Port Erin.

Top: the new style of buffer stop. Compare this with the older fabrications, above and below.

Above: a robust example of stop block which used to be at Port Erin. I have never been able to establish whether the very corroded wrought iron uprights were recycled from a bridge or if they were purpose-built. They support a very heavy timber cross beam.

Below: another example, also at Port Erin.

Above: an IoMR water column, at Port Erin, which still retains the bag. Two similar columns were once to be found on the centre road at Douglas.

Below: one of the few original track infrastructure items remaining in the present Douglas station, this all-timber buffer which at one time would have been at the end of the Ramsey and Peel arrival platform. The brick flower bed and the white picket fence have also been added in more recent years.

Signs of the times

Signs and notices can give a distinct character to any undertaking and are details to be noted. The IoMR has in its long history employed quite a range of styles, making for interesting variety.

Station nameboards varied from place to place. From before Ailsa up until at least the early 1980s, they were painted in red and cream, like the coaching stock, in a plain sans serif font with no shading. The posts were less standardised, being painted either dark green, red, cream, or white, depending on the finish around the individual station buildings.

Above: No.4 Loch leaving Ballasalla in 1976, during the short line period. The station nameboard was then mounted on white posts.

Right: by way of contrast, the nameboard at Ballasalla in 2003 - the colours almost exactly reversed and with added shading. By this time, any consistent style for station nameboards had completely disappeared - in fact, almost every station on the Port Erin line had a different colour board. This also appears to be the case for paint finishes on the station buildings.

Below left: the current board at Santon is in similar style to Port St. Mary, but on red rather than white posts. Note the now almost compulsory flagpole and IoMR flag. The white flower bed behind the nameboard was once the plinth for the grounded E van used as the goods shed here.

Top: one oddity was Ronaldsway Halt, opened in 1967 during the Ailsa period to attract business away from the buses and taxis that served the airport. No more than a piece of ground and a station nameboard, the board had coach red posts, and originally the name was in plain red lettering on a white background, within a black frame.

Above: the current nameboard at Port St.Mary dark maroon with pale cream sans serif lettering and black shading - quite dark compared with the 1960s version.

Below: some of the Ramsey and Peel line station nameboards had dark green lettering with no serifs or shading on a cream background with dark green posts and frames, as seen in this 1950s view of Crosby.
Photo: the late David Odabashian.

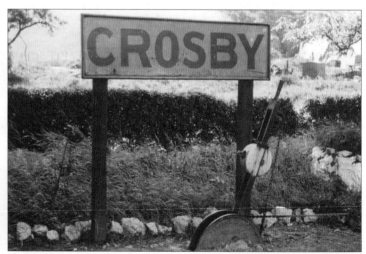

Left: both of the entrance or gate pillars to Douglas station still boast the original IoMR initials in scroll form on a deep red background and gold leaf finish, a fine example of Victorian elegance. This insignia could at one time be found on a wide variety of surfaces including carriage mirrors and the like.

Top: direction sign at Douglas.

Above: this sign has hung in the paint shop at Douglas for as long as I can remember, right back to the early 1970s. It must have come from somewhere on the lines closed by then, and seems typical of the more rural stopping points.

Below: an appropriate sign warns pedestrians of the presence of No.11 Maitland at Port Erin in the 1980s. This gate protects the public right-of-way that crosses the station site, effectively dividing it in two; the main platform, once double sided, even has a dip halfway along its length.

Above: the nameboards at Port Erin have for many years also featured the town name in Manx Gaelic. This particular sign is on the side of the engine shed that faces the platform.

Below: the current Castletown signs are similar to those that formerly existed on the Peel line, though the cream is a little lighter and the lettering has the addition of mid-grey shading.

Chapter 8

Landscape and road traffic

The railway in the wider environment: often it is the setting as much as specific features that may inspire modelling, yet this can be the most difficult aspect to capture in limited spaces.

The scenery

Many railway modellers, not least for lack of space, are forced to ignore the environment away from the railway track or station site, which is a shame.

The IoMR was built to narrow gauge because the terrain was not suitable for standard gauge, so it is worth looking at the landscape, picking out landmarks and features of interest that can give a potential layout the local character and atmosphere.

Sometimes a rare opportunity arises to model more than the immediate surroundings of the railway, more than the thin strip of railway land. When this is possible, taking in the environment and researching it is just as important as getting the railway infrastructure right. This can improve the quality of backscenes, buildings, roads, fauna, period dress, other forms of transport, and industry.

I also find it interesting to look out the local culture, as when exhibiting there is always someone who wants to know about the place in question.

The Isle of Man or Ellan Vannin is 33 miles long by 13 miles wide and at its highest point (Snaefell summit) some 2,036' above sea level. The island sits proudly in the middle of the Irish Sea and is surrounded by the mythical Mannanan's Cloak, belonging to the Celtic Neptune. On many summer days one must actually travel through Mannanan's Cloak when travelling to the island by ship, as a thick

Above: Keristal Bank at the top of the climb out of Douglas. The line here swings sharply to the right and then left into Port Soderick station. The unusual train formation seen here, three engines coupled together, No.1 Sutherland *hauling No.9* Douglas *and No.6* Peveril, *was a special photographic run.*

Below: almost from the opening of the Port Erin line in 1874 until the outbreak of hostilities in 1939, Port Soderick was a mecca for holidaymakers. The station building itself was probably the

largest wayside station on any British narrow gauge railway, and contained a licensed cafeteria.

From the station one could walk through a pleasant wooded glen down to the shore where a hotel and Victorian amusement arcades existed. In 1898 a funicular railway up the cliff was opened which led to a standard gauge tramway along the Marine Drive back to Douglas Head.

The Isle of Man Railway operated special trains from Douglas terminating at Port Soderick. Today it is a quiet cove; little remains but for some architectural infrastructure.

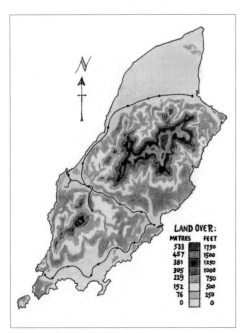

Above: Map showing principal contours of the island.
Drawn by Edwin Lambert.

LAND OVER:

METRES	FEET
533	1750
457	1500
381	1250
305	1000
229	750
152	500
76	250
0	0

sea mist followed by the island suddenly appearing like magic. The island is in the Gulf Stream which has a diverse effect on weather, climate, wildlife, and flora.

Despite its size, the Isle of Man is an island full of dramatic environmental contrasts, in terms of geology, architecture, flora and fauna.

Geologically, the island has a solid mountainous central section, which is formed of slate and granite rock. Much of this area contains natural resources of lead and silver, which resulted in mines at Laxey and around - Foxdale. Laxey had its own harbour for transporting the products away, but Foxdale, being well inland, eventually required a railway to take the output to Ramsey for shipment.

Around the coast there is a vast difference in scene, extremely dramatic in places. From red sandstone cliffs at Peel, clay and sand north of and including Ramsey, and black volcanic rock from Castletown to Port Erin. These rock and stone differences make for many variations in colour and building styles around the island.

With the exception of the land around the 'curraghs' in the northwest of the island leading to Ramsey, the railways were on far from level ground. The Manx Northern route was the most difficult, with two deep glens to cross and the notorious Donkey Bank, which was forever slipping nearer the sea.

The steep line up to Port Soderick from Douglas is another a good example.

From east to west the Peel line followed a natural wide break in the mountain range and the course of the Rivers Dhoo, Greeba, and Neb.

Vegetation

It is quite common to find palm trees growing almost anywhere on the island, and stations were popular places for them to be planted for ornamental purposes. They are commonly called 'cabbage trees' (cordyline australis).

Because the climate is influenced by the Gulf Stream, the growing season is slightly different from most of the United Kingdom. This is significant for modelling as the type of plants will vary, and their colour at any given time of year: many varieties will leaf early, with primroses starting the season by appearing in March. June sees wild orchids growing. The wetland areas around the 'curraghs' near Ballaugh and the Sulby River have flora and fauna of their own. In August, wild fuchsias start to bloom which can be seen almost anywhere from railway cuttings to hedgerows.

September is the most colourful of the summer months: the hills and mountains are covered in a most amazing display of purple heather and yellow gorse.

With so many ways to reproduce different types of tree now in model form, it would not be impossible to display any of the species. Some common types appear around the island such as the pine, larch, beech, sycamore, horse and sweet chestnut, oak and ash. Many of the glens have varieties not seen growing naturally elsewhere on the island - trees such as holm oak, lime, alder, elm, and Corsican pine. These Corsican pines exist in

Glen Mooar and Glen Wyllin, and today they tower over the 75' piers of the Glen Mooar viaduct.

The Forestry Commission has huge plantations of pine for the commercial production of softwood. These can be found on the southern hills near the Peel line (Rhenny and Archallagan), the Slieau Whallian mountains in which the Foxdale line once ran, and the western slopes of the mountains around Ballaugh and Sulby. These plantations contain Sitka and Norway spruce, Japanese larch, lodgepole, and Corsican and Scots pines. Firs are represented by the Douglas, noble and grand varieties.

The glens are naturally deeply wooded areas, generally with some form of water, either a stream, river, or in some cases deep waterfalls. Many are not far from closed and existing railway lines and are worth a look for dramatic lineside scenery.

In the past few years there has been an increase in the placing of animals on model railways, made easier by the availability of numerous whitemetal castings. However, one should be aware that what we consider as normal wildlife in the United Kingdom is not so on the Isle of Man. The island has no foxes, otters, badgers, squirrels, or snakes - and many more creatures too small to model!

What it does have is an abundance of sea birds, notably the Manx shearwater, slightly smaller than a seagull. Wild swans are quite commonly found in harbours and for those including the sea in their landscape, a basking shark would not be out of place. Grey seals are extremely common around the island, especially on the western and southern coasts. One must not forget the Manx cat that has no tail!

Agricultural livestock is now basically the same as on the mainland, but until the 18th century the island had its own breeds of many types of farm animal. One that is still extant is its own four-horn sheep, the Loaghtan.

Above: palm trees were a feature on more than one IoMR station. These four fine examples are at Santon on the south line. Sulby Glen on the Ramsey line was another notable location.

Below: in recent years it has been possible to walk almost the entire length of the closed Peel line. The railway followed a natural valley across the island following the courses of the Dhoo, Greeba, and Neb rivers, which the line crossed in several places. The mountainous environment is very dramatic. This view is near Glen Vine, between Union Mills and Crosby, looking towards Peel.

With a few exceptions all the beaches on the island are of pure sand and very few stones.

Up to the 1980s, entertainments such as 'Punch and Judy' could be seen on many beaches.

Left: Port Erin harbour, beach and Bradda Head. The purple heather on the hillside gives this landmark added atmosphere. In late spring yellow gorse adds to the picture. The local stone cottages have their colour picked out well in the sunlight. Note that the roof slates are not plain grey, but have many tones of blue, purple, and green.

Below: Bradda Head crowned by Milners Tower is just one of many notable landmarks on the island but probably the most noticeable one to the railway traveller as it can be seen from the train window almost directly on leaving Castletown. This 1960 view shows the approach to Port Erin, with the headland in full view.
Photo: the late David Odabashian.

Bottom left: a broad view of the island from the top of Bradda Head. In the foreground is the village of Port Erin; close behind is Port St.Mary; and to the far left is Castletown, once the capital of the island. The land to seaward in the distance includes the island's main airport, Ronaldsway, developed by the RAF in the Second World War. All the runways on the island were built using spoil from the Foxdale mines, and a layout set in this period would allow many workings to Castletown or Ronaldsway.

Local landmarks

The railway and the environment beyond the fence offer a range of possibilities for setting a layout in a specific scenic context. The following may prompt further investigation.

Port Erin line

Port Soderick - glen adjacent to the station and Crogga River. Port Soderick bay was quite a tourist attraction, with a cliff railway until the late 1940s, and amusement arcades (which dated back to Victorian times) until 1947. The spacious station here once contained refreshment rooms.

Ballasalla - the ruins of Rushen Abbey are just a short distance from railway.

Castletown - Silverburn River leading to the harbour. Castle Rushen, former seat of Tynwald and Heads of Mann.

Port Erin - a small harbour within a curved shoreline and beach. Bradda Head can be seen for miles with Milners Tower at its head.

Most stations on the surviving south line (namely Santon, Ballasalla, and Castletown) now have platforms, which did not exist until very recently. Ballasalla station has been completely modernised and is very out of character with the old IoMR Class Three building that once stood on the other side of the line.

Castletown station has had the grand wooden balcony style canopy and platform shelter removed.

Sadly, some stations have been 'adorned' with brightly-coloured modern bus shelters. So, if your preference is for historical interest and not current operation, do avoid the above!

Peel line

Braddan - the unique station/halt which was only open on Sundays had an extremely long ground level gravel platform. Braddan Bridge crosses over the railway which forms part of the TT course (Braddan Corner) with Braddan Church near by.

Crosby - St.Trinian's Church ruins, away from the railway.

St.John's - Foxdale River with the Foxdale railway viaduct to the south, St.John's Church, and Tynwald Hill. Sand pits existed between the railway station and the Foxdale line embankment, with a 3' gauge tramway system within.

Peel - tidal harbour next to the station with Peel Castle at the mouth of River Neb and harbour. Peel Hill on the opposite side of the river from the station, allows for possible inclusion of Corrins Hill and its monument. Herring and kipper factories surrounding the station - there is a challenge for anyone to reproduce the constant smell!

The Foxdale branch

Waterfalls - a very small halt with a minute wooden station building. This station clung to the edge of Slieau Whallian Mountain. A waterfall was crossed by the railway on a simple plate girder bridge.

Foxdale - until the turn of the 19th century, massive mine workings with 3' gauge overhead tramways, washing floors, and associated buildings. After 1905 massive spoil heaps existed for many decades around the station site with the mine buildings in ruins.

Top right: the Foxdale line ran out of St.John's (West) up a sharp curving embankment to take it up and over the IoMR Douglas to Peel railway. This 1950s view shows the line intact despite being closed to passengers since 1940.

Rght: Peel station in July 1956, with a short train about to depart for Douglas.
Both photos: the late David Odabashian.

Below: Peel quay seen from the roof of Peel station shows how Peel castle dominates the harbour and city.

Left: from St.Germains to Bishops Court, south of Ballaugh, the Manx Northern line hugged the coast with some magnificent views. The landscape is far from flat and in places the line ran very close to the cliff edge.
This picture was taken from the trackbed just south of Gob-y-Deigan. In the background is Corrins Hill and St.Patrick's Island, site of St.Germains Cathedral within Peel Castle.

The Ramsey line

All stations on this line were backed to the east by views of the high mountains with plantations, with the sea in the other direction. Station buildings were all on the landward side of the line.

Peel Road - in the early days of this station's existence, a 2' gauge roadside tramway existed (horse power!) to a quarry at Ballavolley.

Donkey Bank - at Gob-y-Deigan, a very dramatic embankment and coastline next to the railway.

Glen Mooar - 75' high three-span viaduct across the glen. Very wooded with stream through leading to a high waterfall named Spooyt Vane, one of the highest falls on the island. Extremely mountainous to the east.

Glen Wyllin - 60' high three-span viaduct under which was the railway-owned amusement park. Extremely mountainous to the east. This glen probably has the most varied collection of trees anywhere on the island - excellent for modelling variation.

Bishops Court - a small halt built for the use of the Bishop of Sodor. Again, dramatic coastline with a small ground level halt without buildings but complete with signal. Some station fittings were added during the railway's existence.

Sulby Bridge - the line hugs the Sulby River which is crossed by a superb 'basket' bridge, the only one of its kind on the island. It was rebuilt around the same time as the two viaducts.

Above the west beach with sea defences at the foot of the Glen. Nearly every piece of wood is different in shape, size, and placing.

Below: Glen Wyllin as it was (left) and as it is (right). The glen was purchased by the IoMR, and

the Company set about building amusement arcades, a boating lake, a bowling green, swings and slides, and refreshment rooms within the Glen, under the viaduct crossing the valley. There was also access to the beach.
Both these views are from the viaduct - that on

the left (by the late David Odabashian) looking northwest (seaward) is dated May 1953 and gives some idea of what the park would have looked like in railway days. Today the glen is a campsite and the picture below (looking inland) highlights the magnificent landscape surrounding the area.

Right: for anyone modelling Manx Northern Railway stations on the northern plains, such as Sulby Glen, Sulby Bridge, Lezayre, or Ramsey, which are all within this view from the Snaefell mountain road, note that the top of the island is almost flat.

The station buildings on the MNR section were all built on the south/east side of the line, so depending on the viewing point you either have a vast flat plain behind or a very mountainous background, which could include views of Snaefell and the massive tree plantations on the side of Slieau Dhoo.

The mountains on the horizon in this picture are part of the Mull of Galloway in Scotland.

Below right: possibly the only structure on the north line not built from Peel sandstone is this overbridge near Kirk Michael.

This section of line was well known for being snowed in during winter months and the rescue of trains was a regular occurrence. The route is popular with walkers during the summer months.

Ramsey - had a large railway area with an expanse of goods sidings leading to the harbour quay line. This was where the output of the Foxdale mines was loaded onto ships, and coal and other incoming items were unloaded.

I also found many tourist brochures useful for researching the surrounding environment.

Having discussed the natural environment, we should turn to the man-made side of the Manx landscape. This too will have an effect on the scenery around the railway and ultimately the operation of the line.

The industrial landscape naturally affected what the railway carried in its freight business.

In the railway's heyday, the most important industry was tourism, with the accompanying accommodation, entertainment, and transportation around the island. This industry was followed closely by agriculture and fishing, not just for the home market but also for export.

Harbours, of which there are many around the island, nearly all had fishing fleets, and there would be many vessels visiting from Ireland or Scotland as well as the Manx fleet depositing a catch. Port Erin, Castletown, Peel, and Ramsey all had harbours that were part of the railway scene. Most have distinctive lighthouses.

Shipbuilding and associated activities with small boats, schooners, and fishing vessels were also a significant industry by the mid-1800s at Peel, Castletown, and Douglas.

Many of the disused mines in the Foxdale area still exist almost complete in architectural terms and would enhance any model of the location.

Brick making was carried out at several places on the island - Ballacorey, Andreas (until 1926), and Glenfaba in Peel. Glenfaba had its own quarry and a plateway system crossed the IoMR at one point. This works remained open until 1965.

Smaller industries included paper making, cotton mills at St.John's, and a potato business at Sulby, later Lezayre, which also produced starch.

At one point around a hundred breweries existed on the island, Castletown probably being the most famous Manx business.

Below: crofters' cottages were once a common form of housing all over the island from the 19th century, and would be an ideal feature on any IoMR/MNR layout. They use an unusual thatching method, being tied down with stringers to stone or wooden pegs fixed into the upper part of the wall. These pegs can be clearly seen in the nearest dwelling. These particular cottages are at Cregneash in the south of the island; others can be found to the north of Ramsey.

Road traffic

Although the European Parliament passed a common statute in 1967 for road sign styles across Europe, as with all things political, this had to pass through the Manx House of Keys and Tynwald before becoming law on the island, so many of the old black & white cast iron signs, red triangles, red circles with black & white poles persisted for quite some time after this date.

Roads on the TT races course should have the curb stones painted alternately black and white.

The number plates on motor vehicles until recent years came in two basic variations - MN and a four-figure number, e.g. MN 1234, or AMN and a three-figure number, e.g. AMN 123. Up until the 1970s it would be fair to say that the type of vehicle, whether private or commercial, was likely to be much older than on the mainland.

The bus company

A common but still interesting feature in the environment of many model railway stations seems to be the bus! The Isle of Man should be treated no differently. Port Erin station, terminus of the south line, has for many decades incorporated a bus depot.

The island's railways, like so many in the United Kingdom, were suffering loss of business to the many companies offering road transport. By the late 1920s the IoMR had apparently taken enough of a beating. It purchased the competition and formed Isle of Man Road Services, so the railway company effectively served the whole island one way or another. The buses were naturally operated to

the benefit of the railway! The exception was in Douglas, where the Corporation buses operated alongside those of the Road Services.

The early vehicles were single deck, many being cast-offs from companies across the water, until the arrival of the first double decker in 1946.

Once the IoMR had formed the Isle of Man Road Services bus company, there was but one other operator, Douglas Corporation, which worked within the confines of the town. A Corporation bus could nearly always be seen in the forecourt of Douglas station to meet an incoming railway service.

The IoM Road Services and Douglas Corporation Transport survived separately until 1976 when Manx National Transport was formed.

Many ancient vehicles were still in use until the late 1970s but both operations now have a very modern fleet.

Coach tour companies flourished right from the start of motorised road transport, and many companies existed - Highlander, Corkhills, Mona's Queen, Stanley Motors, Broadway Coaches, and many others. At the

Left: a railway-owned 32-seat Bedford OWB of 1945, with Duple utility saloon bodywork, in Isle of Man Road Services livery at the old Port Erin bus depot in the 1950s.
Photo: the late David Odabashian.

Below left: a 1945 Bedford OWB with Duple bodywork, fleet number 27, registration number GMN 146, at Port Erin in 1956. In true IoMR fashion this vehicle was recycled when its days as a bus were finished and converted in 1966 into a railway parcels delivery van, No.118.

Below: Harris promenade, Douglas, with a 1950 Bedford OB, fleet no.43, LMN 546. This bus was also rebuilt as parcels van No.121 in 1967.

Photos: David Warren.

turn of the 19th century some magnificent charabancs were operated by individuals and small companies to and from many destinations including those made popular by the Victorian visitors.

Douglas Corporation Transport started by being responsible for the horse trams and the Victoria Road cable tramway. Its first buses were delivered in 1914. The services were confined to the Borough of Douglas. Like the Isle of Man Road Services, it was amalgamated into Manx National Transport in 1976.

Left: two Leyland Titans of 1949 at Douglas bus station in 1975. The front vehicle is fleet No.9, KMN 517. Note the yellow & red Corporation bus in the background.

Right: a 1963 Leyland Titan with Northern Counties bodywork, fleet No.57, one of the many secondhand imports to the island. This vehicle was built for Stratford Blue and acquired from Midland Red in 1972. Note the change of logo between this and the view opposite.

Both photos: David Warren.

Above: Douglas Corporation 8122 MN, a 1964 AEC Regent 5 with MCCW bodywork. The vehicle is seen at Derby Castle, terminus of the MER.

Below: fleet No.90, a Leyland PSUI/13, NMN 908, at Lord Street, Douglas, in 1956. Note the revised Isle of Man Railway crest on the front of this vehicle - Mannin has been replaced by a Road Services bus.

Above: preserved fleet No.64, KMN 835, a 1949 AEC Regent III with a Northern Counties body, is seen in Castletown in 2000 on an excursion. These vehicles could still be seen in service around Douglas into the 1970s.

Below: probably one of the most utilised vehicles on the island in the 1970s was the 1964 Leyland PD3A/1. Fleet No.68, 68 UMN, is seen at the now demolished Lord Street bus station in Douglas in July 1975.
Photos: David Warren.

Chapter 9

Museum pieces and other curios

It could be argued that all of the surviving IoMR is a museum, with historic artefacts on show and in use, but there is much more preserved and displayed in museums or to be seen elsewhere.

Although there have been decades of destruction by deliberate decision as well as just plain vandalism, many items from the railway's past have fortunately been 'retained', the term I prefer to use. Some significant items have been saved and put on display for future generations and railway enthusiasts to appreciate, in various parts of the British Isles as well as on the island.

The most obvious place on the island is the railway-owned museum at Port Erin, which generally houses at least two redundant locomotives plus the Governor's Saloon F75 and the Royal Coach F36. Modellers can also research many smaller items here.

Relics may very well have been moved or simply left in odd corners. Even those formally on display may not be correctly identified and labelled, but at least they have been preserved for posterity and are available for inspection.

Right and below: No.3 Pender now resides in the Museum of Science and Industry, Manchester. This engine was built in 1873 as the last of the initial batch of three for the railway. It was to be called Viking but the name was changed during construction. It was withdrawn from service in 1959 and put on display with the other redundant locomotives.

In 1979 it left the island to return to its birthplace in Manchester. In 1980 it was sectioned to show the working parts of a steam engine. Whilst this was being done it was found to be in a very bad state and had obviously not been withdrawn from service until well after it had started to deteriorate. A two foot long spanner was found in the boiler barrel whilst this work was being carried out!

Pender is presented in its final form, with the larger boiler and side tanks rather than the small type as first delivered. The complete side of the machine has been finished in almost original condition, albeit in a suspiciously dark Brunswick green with vermilion-black-vermilion lining.

Photographed by courtesy of the
Museum of Science and Industry, Manchester.

For dedicated enthusiasts, the Douglas workshops are full of history, but it must be remembered that this is a working environment and it is not possible just to walk in. Prior permission to visit is required in writing from the Director of Transport.

The Narrow Gauge Museum at Tywyn in Wales houses a number of signalling items.

Right: No.16 Mannin *on a running-in trip up the Douglas Promenade! This was actually a wooden replica of the engine made by the railway staff for use in the Douglas Carnival some years past.*

Below: the 'Lump', as it was not so affectionately called by engine crews. This was the square cab top fitted to No.12 Hutchinson *in 1980, with that blue paintwork.*

Below right: the discarded original side tanks from No.1 Sutherland, *seen in 1998.*

Below: the small snowplough, built in Douglas to fit any of the locos, back or front. It was simply attached to the loco by means of four bolts onto the buffer beams. There was a larger plough for No.15 Caledonia *which could only be installed on the front of that engine.*

Below right: the ceremonial shield and flags will be recognised by many. They were used for almost any special event the old company could justify. More recent occasions were the 1967 reopening, the 1973 railway centenary, and the 1974 south line centenary. The flags, up to five in number, were often changed from being all Isle of Man to a mixture of members of the Commonwealth or the countries that constitute the United Kingdom.

The shield was fixed to the front of the locomotive's chopper coupling.

Top left: No.1 Sutherland *not long before the loco was taken away for overhaul in 1996. Many historic artefacts surround No.1, including one of the small snowploughs and a shield headboard with the customary flags.*

Below left: No.1 Sutherland *was in 1975 one of the first locomotives to be put on display in the museum.*

F75, the coach behind, includes the body of an original four-wheel coach, A12, which was used by the island's governor, Sir Henry Loch, and the Duke of Sutherland for the railway's opening in 1873; A12 was paired with C9.

Below: *these fine concrete Victorian vases can still be found in many places around the IoMR system. Most, if not all, were originally intended for use as brick pillar capitals, adorning stations such as Port Erin. Today they decorate the platforms. This particular example is at Douglas.*

Below left: *platform benches varied from station to station. Many were of the solid timber type but this original IoMR example is of cast iron with timber slats. The source and date of manufacture are unknown but these seats were still common in the 1960s. This particular one is on Douglas station.*

At one time there was a 'best kept station' award seat, but I have not seen it for many years, since trains last ran to Peel.

Below: *parcel and luggage sack trolley.*

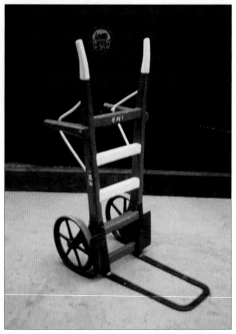

THE ISLE OF MAN RAILWAY

Right: No.16 Mannin - the last of the Manx Peacocks, the last steam engine to be purchased by the IoMR, the largest and most powerful Beyer,Peacock on the island, built in 1926, and withdrawn in 1964. Locked up in the museum in front of F36, the royal saloon, No.16 Mannin was during the late 1970s displayed in an unlined Indian red livery.

Below: the collection of clutter in front of the stop block is as interesting as the block itself!

This is a prize example of how odd bits of railway history can pop up just about anywhere, especially on a narrow gauge system. I had previously seen this pony truck on the back of a very sad and broken M wagon in Douglas yard. It appeared again here in Port Erin some years later. It is in fact one of the few remains of locomotive No.2 Derby of 1873, which was dismantled and scrapped in 1951.

Below: this might be seen as a railway junk pile, but of course it is not junk at all. Like any self-respecting hoarder, the railway never likes to throw anything away. The benefit of having a standardised locomotive fleet is that many parts will generally fit almost any loco, so here we have just a small section of the parts store that has built up over the last 130 years or so.

Quite some history, then, and it may possibly even include items from the two dismantled engines, Derby and Tynwald.

The machine in front is the old stationary steam engine which used to drive, via a belt system, the workshop machinery. This is now all done by electricity.

Chapter 10

Redundant locomotives

Even before the Peel and Ramsey lines closed and traffic levels fell, the railway had more locos than it needed, or could afford to maintain. The sad sight of redundant locos inspired me to model them.

Above: a line-up of redundant locomotives in need of new boilers and major overhauls was originally to be seen at St.John's station. However, when the Peel line was closed in 1968 this 'display' was moved to the former Peel line departure platform at Douglas. Locomotives (in order) are No.14 Thornhill, *No.3* Pender, *No.1* Sutherland, *and No.16* Mannin. *No.15* Caledonia *was also here, but for some reason No.5* Mona *was put on display at Port Erin.*

The palms always looked splendid in the centre road garden, and the stationmaster at this time maintained plenty of hanging baskets on the Port Erin platform and around the station entrance to complement the display. How different Douglas station looks with the platform canopies.

No.14 Thornhill *was the only Beyer,Peacock locomotive supplied to the Manx Northern Railway, having been built alongside IoMR No.7* Tynwald *at the Gorton Foundry in 1880. No.3 on the MNR, it was incorporated into the IoMR as No.14. Spending most of its working life on the Peel and Ramsey lines, the engine was withdrawn in 1963, like so many, with a weak boiler. Consequently,* Thornhill *was stored with the others in the carriage shed, awaiting the overhaul which never happened.*

Thornhill *is no longer on the railway but is privately preserved on the island.*

Left: No.1 Sutherland *seen in 1974 through the rear cab spectacle of No.3* Pender. *In recent years* Sutherland *has been returned to traffic, whilst* Pender *is displayed in the Museum of Science and Industry in Manchester, sectioned to show the workings of a steam locomotive.*

Right: a 1974 view of No.9 Douglas standing on the original Port Erin departure platform in Douglas, still in the 'Ailsa' green livery it was given for display. No.9 was put here in a bid to raise funds for its restoration.

Built in 1896, No.9 Douglas was withdrawn in 1953. It stands here almost identical to the day it was delivered to the island, with small boiler, Salter safety valves, and the builder's plate intact.

Sheltering under the iron and glass canopies of Douglas station, the locomotive is in front of the corrugated screen that partitioned the goods shed from the passenger station.

Middle right: in 1998 when No.1 Sutherland was so beautifully restored for the 125th anniversary of the Isle of Man Railway, it was always known that the locomotive was to run only for a limited period as the boiler had been borrowed - for three years - from Fenella. In fact that loan was to last some four years.

No.1 was first outshopped in a spring green livery and later received the Indian red introduced for the whole fleet (except Caledonia).

It is admired by many and as the first of the IoMR Beyer,Peacocks dating back to 1873 it holds quite a place in the railway's history. In this May 2003 view, Sutherland has given up the borrowed boiler and stands within the running shed at Douglas in pieces, its future uncertain.

Unfortunately it is not just a case of replacing the boiler and water tanks. Sutherland has some very serious defects as a result of age and wear and tear, and restoration would cost in the region of £200,000.

Behind Sutherland is No.11 Maitland, a stalwart of the running fleet for many decades. Maitland too is now at the point where her boiler is at the end of its useful life, and a major overhaul is required.

Below right: everything one might need for a steam engine except tanks, a boiler, and a firebox - the frames and other parts of Kissack are seen in the carriage workshops in 2001, all a lot tidier and more together than the last time I saw them, some two years previously. However, many parts had been borrowed from this loco 'kit'! Happily, this engine was subsequently sent to England to be rebuilt and rejoined the running fleet in 2005.

Below: the disembodied chimney from No.8 Fenella languishing in the shed at Douglas.

Left: No.6 Peveril was known on the island as the Peel engine, as it spent most of its working life shedded there. The name has not got such a close connection with railway as most of the other locos in the fleet. Although apparently a popular Manx name, it comes from the novel by Sir Walter Scott, entitled 'Peveril of the Peaks'.

Withdrawn from service in 1960, it was displayed and eventually stored with Mona in the carriage shed.

Below left: in January 1999 the famous corrugated iron carriage shed, which had been standing since the 1880s, was emptied of its treasures and pulled down. Mona once again saw daylight and was moved into the running shed.

Above: in 1974 the Isle of Man Steam Railway Supporters Association began a cosmetic restoration of the engine, seen here outside the steam shed in Douglas. Some small boiler parts are still missing, but otherwise the engine is visually complete, and now resides in the Port Erin museum.

Below: the work carried out in Douglas in 1998/1999 involved major trackwork, moving the signal box, building a new carriage shed, and providing a cover over the open section of track between the running shed and the carriage workshop. Mona is seen during the summer of 1999 in this new covered area. A few days after this photo was taken I witnessed somebody polishing the brass dome - thankfully I am obviously not the only one to love this particular locomotive!

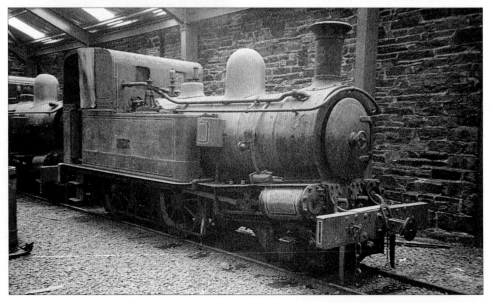

THE ISLE OF MAN RAILWAY

Mona – my favourite Manx locomotive

In 1973 I was a young teenager and (then as now) a member of the Isle of Man Steam Railway Supporters Association. Members were invited to help out on the railway doing odd jobs - polishing, painting, and gardening, to name but a few tasks. Roger Webster, the stationmaster at Douglas, dispatched me to Port Erin with a pass and a pot of very sticky black paint with which to paint the smokebox of No.5 *Mona*, which was on display there having been withdrawn in 1968. It was a task I undertook with great pride.

That was the last time I saw the loco until these pictures were taken in the carriage shed in Douglas during the mid-1990s.

Mona sat neglected in the back of this shed for almost 30 years until the shed was demolished at the turn of the century. As can be seen, it is in a very poor condition.

Below: one of the few colour pictures I was able to take of Mona *in the old carriage shed. The graffiti painted on the tank side reads 'Mona is scrap'.*

Chapter 11

The railcars and the first diesel loco

Internal combustion comes to the railway, in the shape of the two large bogie diesel railcars Nos.19 & 20 acquired from County Donegal, and much later the Schöma diesel No.17 Viking.

For some reason these two railcars, numbered 19 and 20 have an attraction and fascination which is quite different from any other item on the Isle of Man Railway.

They were built for the County Donegal Railways Joint Committee in 1950 and 1951 respectively. The CDR closed just ten years later, on 1st January 1960.

The mechanical parts were constructed by Walker Brothers in Wigan, with the bodywork being made by the Great Northern Railway of Ireland.

They were landed in Douglas in May 1961 and entered service later that year in an attempt to win back business from the bus company - which at that time the railway still owned!

The railcars were articulated and came in two quite separate sections: the driver's cab and front end were mounted on the power unit, while the passenger compartment rested on rear of that unit and was supported at the rear by a non-powered bogie.

When the railcars arrived from Ireland, the CDR couplings were not compatible with the Manx choppers, due to differences in height and shape. During their early days in the 1960s the railcars were run with a G van sandwiched in the middle to accommodate luggage and goods. A number of vans were fitted with vacuum brake pipes and had the couplings altered to match the railcars; G19 was the first. It was to be years before the couplings were actually changed on the railcars themselves.

The two railcars were worked back to back, which caused some initial problems. The transmissions had only one reverse gear and the Gardner 6LW diesel engines and transmissions could not be controlled from the opposite end (i.e. in true multiple unit fashion), and consequently each railcar had to pull the dead weight of the other. On the Port Erin line this caused some severe adhesion problems, so the railcars were used mostly on the Peel and Ramsey routes. A lack of adequate turning facilities precluded them being used singly.

The railcars did not receive official painted Isle of Man Railway fleet numbers until more recent years. Consequently they retained their CDR identities of Nos.19 and 20, which happily did not conflict with any IoMR stock.

There were slight differences in the appearance of the two vehicles, notably the window layout (both in the cab and the passenger saloon) and the livery at the driving ends: No.19 had a triangle painted on the radiator while No.20 had an embossed chevron.

The original red and cream livery style was inherited from the CDR, but around 1977 the two railcars were painted in the darker red and cream of the IoMR coaches, with a black roof.

By 1988 there was a sharp contrast in livery and appearance. They were painted in the red and white livery of the now nationalised bus operator on the island. This was the only time these units received official fleet numbers.

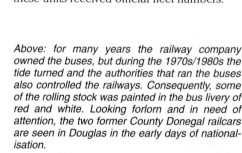

Above: for many years the railway company owned the buses, but during the 1970s/1980s the tide turned and the authorities that ran the buses also controlled the railways. Consequently, some of the rolling stock was painted in the bus livery of red and white. Looking forlorn and in need of attention, the two former County Donegal railcars are seen in Douglas in the early days of nationalisation.

Left: the Walkers diesel railcars, No.19 (nearest) and No.20, at Port Erin. There were slight differences in the appearance of the two vehicles, notably the window layout and the livery at the cab ends.

With this change of livery came about a change of use, to permanent way duties, in an attempt to lighten the use of the steam fleet. This unfortunately took its toll on what were now historic vehicles. It was not until 1992 when the Schöma diesel was purchased that the railcars were virtually taken out of use in a very poor condition, as they were not suitable for passenger work.

In recent years a restoration project has been started, but unfortunately, with the exception of the running gear and chassis, as the material has deteriorated so much, this would have effectively resulted in replicas. The diesel engines and running gear were to be refurbished by the Steam Packet Co., and the bodies were partially rebuilt in the railway works at Douglas. More recently it has been suggested that the power units could be exchanged for new Cummins engines which would allow for multiple unit operation. However, the restoration has been subject to a pause and they have been put into store.

Top: a view of both railcars at Port Erin, No.20 nearest. Note the differences in the cab ends and the body side window fittings.

Centre: the railcars retained their CDR identities as Nos.19 and 20, which conveniently did not clash with any motive power in the Isle of Man Railway roster. They did not carry official fleet numbers until more recent years. The pair, with No.20 leading, is seen on the Port Erin departure platform at Douglas in 1974. The cream chevron design on the cab of this unit was inherited from the CDR livery.

Below: the cab end of No.20, in the entrance of the old carriage shed at Douglas. Adapted IoMR couplings have been fitted. The deterioration is all too clear around the windows and in numerous other places.

Below right: No.19 in the running shed at Douglas in a very poor condition shortly before the units were dismantled. During this period this unit had a large void in the right-hand cab window frame; it was even used in traffic in this condition. The only time these units received official fleet numbers was when they were painted in the bus livery.

Left: seen in the now reduced Douglas station, former County Donegal railcar No.20 heads the pair whilst on shunting duties in 1998. Note the sharp contrast in livery and appearance: the units look unloved and in dire need of attention. The red and white bus livery looks awful. The chevron has gone though the outline can still be made out on the black grille.

I only ever rode in these vehicles once, and only while they were being shunted around Douglas station. The motion was quite odd.

Below: whilst the diesel engines and running gear were being refurbished by the Steam Packet Co., the bodies were rebuilt in the railway workshops at Douglas. The frames for the new cab ends are seen in the covered area between the running shed and paint shop; they have since been clad but remain incomplete.

Above: stripped down to the frames, the original passenger section of No.20 is in the front of this view whilst the new hardwood frame for No.19 sits behind. The corrosion and decay discovered during stripping down meant that these were going to be replicas rather than restorations.

Below: twelve months later, the passenger section exterior is almost complete. No.19 is nearest the camera. This is, unfortunately, as far as the restoration has been taken and work was halted shortly after this photograph

was taken. The units now reside in this condition at the rear of the Douglas carriage shed. These vehicles were to have received the 1961 red and cream livery.

Below: the rebuilt passenger section of No.20. These photographs of the coach bodies under restoration provide a good opportunity to show the interconnecting doorway which exists between the coach body and the driver's cab unit, not easy to see in photographs of the complete units.

THE ISLE OF MAN RAILWAY

A German immigrant

When one thinks of the Isle of Man Railway locomotives, the first thought is not of diesels. The railway had been operated by the fleet of fifteen Beyer, Peacock 2-4-0 side tank locomotives and the sole Dübs 0-6-0T engine.

In 1992 the IoMR purchased secondhand a 900mm gauge four-wheel Schöma diesel hydraulic for shunting, permanent way work (removing the need to use the railcars), and the emergency rescue of trains in the event of a steam loco failure.

Built on 17th June 1958 at the Christoph Schöttler Maschinenfabrik works in Diepholz, near Bremen in northern Germany, as works number 2066, it was delivered to R. Petersen & Co. in Hamburg and worked as No. 208 at the Grube Treue coal mine near Alversdorf. This closed in 1988 and it is assumed that the loco was put into store until sold in 1992.

Weight is 24 tons, and wheelbase 2,200mm. The power unit is a V12 engine delivering some 200 horsepower through hydraulic transmission to both axles.

This was the first locomotive to be added to the roster since the delivery of No.16 Mannin from Beyer, Peacock in 1926. As well as being regauged (from 900 to 914mm), the loco has been fitted with Manx chopper couplings, side chains, and vacuum brakes.

In 1993 it was outshopped in the 1873 livery of Brunswick green, fully lined out in vermilion-black-vermilion, but retaining the bright red running gear below the footplate. On Good Friday 1993 it was named Viking, the name originally intended for No.3, although on this occasion the name was chosen through a competition in local schools.

In 2003 it was repainted into a lighter green livery (though slightly darker than the 'Ailsa' green) with white-black-white lining. The running gear remained red.

The loco still carries its original builder's plates on the cab sides and front radiator. These plates, and the IoMR nameplate, are cast in aluminium and not brass like the steam locos.

Chapter 12

Passenger stock

In relation to its route mileage, the Isle of Man Railway has operated an enormous number of passenger vehicles - at its peak, some ninety coaches - reflecting its principal rôle on the island.

This is not surprising as the railway was built with passenger traffic in mind from the outset, but it was seasonal, involving huge numbers of holidaymakers in the summer months and very little business during the winter.

In high season, it was not unknown for a Port Erin train to leave Douglas with anything up to fourteen bogie coaches, of many different types. Generally, these longer trains were banked at the rear by an additional loco, which would drop off as soon as the train was out of Douglas without any delay to progress.

Ramsey and Peel trains would leave Douglas as one rake, double-headed, and would be split at St.John's.

In 1873, at a time when major railway companies in Britain and around the world were beginning to invest in bogie coaches, the IoMR, through lack of funds, took delivery of their first passenger vehicles, all four-wheelers, from the Metropolitan Carriage and Wagon Company in Birmingham.

In later years, these short coach bodies were 'paired' onto new bogie underframes ordered from Metropolitan, joining the F series as the conversions were carried out.

It was not until 1876 that the company, realising that the railway was a success and moving forward, ordered the first bogie compartment coaches. The first of the F series, as we know them today, F1 to 6, were built by Brown, Marshalls & Co.

Two distinct types of bogie were used. More common was the 4'6" wheelbase fabricated diamond frame. A 4'9" wheelbase pressed steel plate frame was introduced for the 'pairs' chassis. It was not uncommon for them to be swapped around as the plate frames gave a better ride. Both used 2'3" diameter wheels.

Above: a typical mixed rake of IoMR stock, in the modern version of the classic red and cream livery. Nearest the camera is F36, the Royal coach, which is now on display in the museum at Port Erin. All the other saloons of this type have had the seating changed, either to bus style or purpose-built bench seats, both with practically no leg room.

IoMR coach types

Prefix

A three compartment 1st class
B three compartment 2nd class
C guard and two 2nd class compartments
D three compartment 1st/2nd composite
E brake and passenger luggage van
F all bogie stock
N Manx Northern 'Cleminson' vehicles

Below left: C1 or F64. Most if not all the original four-wheel coaches were mounted in 'pairs' on new bogie chassis between 1909 and 1926. Sitting on equally derelict open wagon M69, the body of C1 is pictured in the old carriage shed at Douglas.

Below right: photographed in 1953, IoMR E1 was a passenger luggage and brake van, supplied to the MNR in 1895 as No.19. When built it had guard's duckets on the sides. These vans were either relegated to goods traffic, as here, or turned into grounded goods sheds at stations.
Photo: the late David Odabashian.

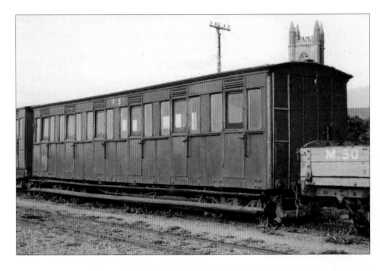

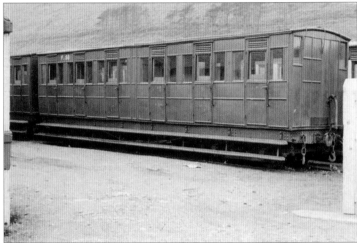

Top: F3, one of six vehicles that formed the first batch of bogie coaches. F1 to F4 were open thirds with one full height partition between the passenger accommodation and the guard's compartment, while F5 and F6 were composites with first and third class compartments. None of these vehicles still exist. The picture was taken at Kirk Michael in August 1955, with the coach in the red/brown livery of the time.

Above: F58 at Peel station in July 1956. Between 1909 and 1926, twenty-five steel underframes were ordered to 'pair' up the bodies of the ageing four-wheeled coaches. The small panel between the originally separate bodies can be clearly seen. The body of F58 was scrapped in 1968 and the underframe used for the ill-fated container service.
Photos: the late David Odabashian.

Below: F54, an original 'pairs' coach, seen in the carriage workshops in 1998, has undergone a total rebuild. The gap between the two old sections has been built out, and the door vents have been matched along the whole length of the coach. The original F54 'pairs' set was the only one with a brake end. Prior to its rebuild, this chassis was used as a permanent way runner.

Top and above: F11 and F18 were two of the smaller F coaches with wooden bodies and frames. These coaches had the body panels carried down over the frames. This was more noticeable when these vehicles were in the red and cream livery as the lower strip is painted black to match the frames of other stock. F11 is seen (above) on the siding in Port Erin in 1996, while F18 seen (top) on a service train at Port Erin in 1995.

Below: in a very sombre purple lake livery, the original MNR colours, F66 stands in Douglas station. One of the few 'pairs' still in service, this set was converted in 1920. Some of the first vehicles mounted together in this way on the new bogie chassis ran for some years with a gap between the two bodies, as the chassis was somewhat longer than the two body sections. All were eventually filled in - the panel can be seen quite clearly.

Some early bogie coaches had wooden underframes while the more modern had steel framed chassis.

Even with the introduction of the bogie coaches, third class travel had not changed at all and remained very spartan with plain wooden benches, whilst second class had at least gained some shape to the back of the seat. First class benefited from the addition of armrests, luggage racks, leather door trim, and curtains.

All stock had wooden panelled exteriors.

Hurst Nelson and the Swansea Wagon Co. were the main suppliers of coaching stock for the Manx Northern Railway.

The island's two railway companies, the Manx Northern and the Isle of Man Railway, were amalgamated in 1905. The IoMR had always had a low opinion of some of the MNR stock because of incidents that occurred on the early through services from Ramsey to Douglas before the amalgamation.

However, the fleet of fourteen Cleminson-underframe six-wheelers of 1879 were somewhat more modern and comfortable than the IoMR's existing four-wheelers. The Cleminsons were eventually given the prefix N and gave a number of years further service on the IoMR until around 1950 when they were put to rest behind the carriage shed at St.John's for many years and forgotten until some fell apart where they stood. Fortunately two of them were saved and have been preserved. One body also escaped by being grounded outside the running shed at Douglas and used as a mess room until recent years.

Top left: N46, one of the six-wheel Cleminson coaches delivered to the Manx Northern in 1879, a standard third class vehicle. Although some were scrapped, several remained in use with the IoMR until the 1950s. Those remaining then were painted in the all red/brown livery. They were not scrapped but hidden away behind St.John's carriage shed until the demolition crew arrived. N46 is seen at St.John's (Foxdale) in June 1954 in the 1917 tan and chocolate livery.
Photo: the late David Odabashian.

Above left: N42, one of only two remaining Manx Northern Railway six-wheel Cleminson coaches, pictured in 1975 at Ballasalla, having not long arrived from St.John's.
I believe this was the only coach rescued from the then closed St.John's carriage shed; it was certainly the only Cleminson to survive the scrapper's torch or vandals. It was cosmetically restored and placed on show at the Port Erin museum for a number of years.

Left: having been removed from the museum, N42 has spent more recent years in the sheds at Douglas. It is seen here in a very faded Manx Northern Railway livery.
It is the only example of the MNR Cleminson coaches still on its original chassis and consequently the only possible candidate for a return to traffic, but underframe is built entirely of timber and one of the main cross members is badly wasted.
The only other Cleminson still in existence is the body that was used as a mess room for loco crews outside the running shed in Douglas. Although removed from the site, the coach body is in store in Douglas.

THE ISLE OF MAN RAILWAY

A few other MNR coaches were taken into IoMR ownership. One was F39, the composite coach built for the Foxdale branch service, which is still in service today although slightly altered externally from its original condition. F39 was converted into a camping coach for the personal use of Lord Ailsa. It was the only coach on the island with a lavatory, kitchen facilities, and a bright yellow and blue livery scheme - the colours of the Ailsa clan. It would make an interesting model to contrast with the normal colour scheme.

Two other former MNR coaches, later given numbers F37 and F38, were the most modern bogie coaches on the island with steel underframes and well-fitted compartments, including electric lighting; they became a pattern for future IoMR stock.

With the increase in route mileage, new vehicles were required, and came in batches from Brown, Marshalls & Co., Metropolitan Carriage and Wagon Co., and Ashbury.

The saloons were delivered in 1905 and considered very modern for their time. The first class sections in F35 and F36 were even grander than anything before, both in terms of upholstery and finish of the partition panels, which were made from polished sycamore and mahogany. F36, the 'Royal Saloon', can now be seen in the Port Erin museum.

All but a couple of these saloons are still in service although much altered internally.

The last new passenger vehicle, F49, was a three compartment half brake, built by Metropolitan in 1926.

It is important for modellers to note that after 1925 all coaches with brake compartments ran with the brake at the Douglas end, but this is not the case today.

In the saloons, the third class passenger had at last gained cushions although they were fitted to tram-style reversible seats, which allowed very little leg room.

Top right: F39, the Foxdale, or Kitto's, coach, as this vehicle has been called over the years, built for the Manx Northern Railway in 1897 as No.17. It was renumbered 15 in 1899 and later became IoMR F39. It is shorter than most Manx coaches, and has slightly different bogies. This coach was used mainly for the limited passenger traffic on the Foxdale branch. The name 'Kitto's coach' derives from the captain of the Foxdale lead mines whose family used the only first class compartment in the coach. Lord Ailsa had it converted into a camping coach for his own use.
The coach was repainted in the purple lake livery for the MNR centenary.
This picture from 2001 shows F39 at the back of the steam shed in Douglas. It had been recently restored to the red and cream livery, and was receiving attention to one of the bogies, which is why it is at an odd angle.

Above right: F39 pictured in 1979 in the carriage workshop awaiting varnishing having been overhauled. The guard's duckets have been glazed for passenger use.

Right: third class accommodation in the 1905 saloons. These tram style reversible seats were considered far from comfortable, and seating capacity was less than normal compartment stock. The modern seating in the saloons cannot be considered to be any better!
Photo: the late David Odabashian.

In fact, coach interiors have varied considerably, both between the classes and over time, from the sumptuous comforts of first class to third class coaches almost totally devoid of any aid to comfort.

The early four-wheel A series first class coaches were very plush, having individual blue cloth cushions and buttoned backrests up to head level.

Travellers in the B, C, and D series, the 'lower class' coaches, were not so lucky: they generally had plain wooden benches.

Train comfort has come a little way on the island. All rolling stock is now fitted with some kind of seat cushion. My children found it quite good fun to ride in some of the older 'pairs' coaches which in the 1990s still only had thin cushions on the bench and not on the back rest. For travellers in the days when the track was in dire need of repair, the ride must have been quite an uncomfortable experience.

Different coloured fabrics have been use at different periods - greys, black, and Indian red/maroon for third class, while rich blue was a popular colour for first class.

Most of the material currently used for seating is in mid grey, with the exception of the saloons, which have brown leatherette, on modern replacement plywood seats.

Woodwork is generally wood-grained paint effect or, in the case of some of the recent rebuilds, varnished hardwood.

For the different periods, it is worth checking for interior detail from a photo.

The saloons, of which there are three basic types, originally had tram style seating and were not especially comfortable. Around 1975 these coaches were fitted with bus windows and modern replacement plywood seats, with brown leatherette cushions. Legroom in these coaches is limited - well worth remembering when trying to fit all the required seats into a model.

Wood partitions in most coaches were and are generally light orange/yellow pine wood-grained paint effect or, in the case of some of the recent rebuilds, varnished hardwood. Others were painted cream.

Most compartments had three picture frames above the seats, with views of the island that could be seen from or reached by the railway.

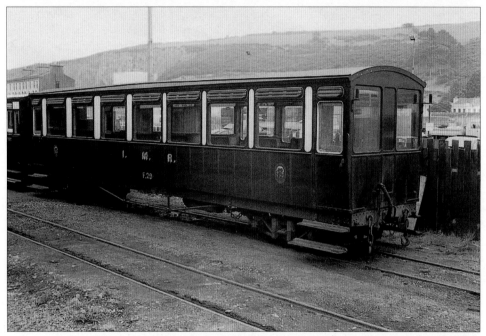

Top and above left: F29. Eight of these saloons were built for the IoMR in 1905 with various internal arrangements. The first six had all third accommodation in open compartments, with tram style reversible seats. F35 and F36 had two first class open compartments with superb blue fabric armchair seats and wooden interior panelling.

Left: F26. This and F25 have all third class accommodation with seat height partitions, giving the equivalent of five third class open sections and a guard's compartment. During the 1970s the railway authorities saw fit to install bus windows in place of the originals, but fortunately they have all since been removed.

THE ISLE OF MAN RAILWAY

Door handles! How many of us have spent hours trying to solder model door handles on straight? Closer inspection of photos of Manx coaches reveals that many handles do not sit true on a closed door, so it is perfectly correct to solder them at an angle!

Electric lighting was fitted to all existing F series coaches from 1911, with a dynamo providing power, to replace the existing oil lamps. Coaches delivered after this date came fitted with electric lighting from new.

Vehicles equipped with electric lighting can be identified either by a plank down the middle of the roof covering the wires or what appears to be a row of stitching down the centre of the roof. Three wires dropped over both coach ends to terminal sockets. Ceramic or wooden caps were placed over the roof entry into the light fittings.

The lighting systems suffered from a lack of maintenance and by the Ailsa period in the 1960s any lighting available for use was powered from car batteries.

Ventilators existed on the roof of all vehicles from new, in various types and forms. As far as the modern fleet is concerned, these roof vents started to disappear from the 1950s.

There was, after the accident in 1925 in which *Pender* went through the buffer stops in Douglas station, and a number of other incidents, a requirement to fit vacuum brakes to the stock. It was a slow process, so it is worth checking photos for evidence of brake pipes on individual coaches. Some vehicles were never so fitted, especially the 'Empress' vans.

It was not until 1937 that steam heating was fitted to coaches and then only to twenty-six vehicles in the fleet. Before this, foot-warmers (which had been obtained secondhand!) were provided for the use of first class passengers only. Some of the locomotives were never fitted with steam heating pipes. The requirement to fit vacuum brakes for train braking may have been a factor in this. The smaller engines must have struggled to find enough steam for hauling the train and stopping it, let alone heating the coaches as well. On the other hand, it was not unknown for trains to leave Douglas without either brake or heating pipes connected, even if they were fitted! One wonders if this was a ploy on the part of the engine crew to save work on the footplate!

Top right: F49, one of the large F series, the last of the half brakes, and the last coach to be delivered to the railway, in 1926. It was supplied with vacuum brakes at a time when not one of the locomotives was so fitted. It is seen here in the 1980s purple lake and off-white.

Above right: a 2004 view of F49 at Douglas, restored to the classic red and cream livery. This is the only remaining coach of this type left in service.

Right: F46 seen in the 1990s, painted in the off-white & purple lake livery applied to vehicles delivered new in the 1920s.

Depletion

Between 1967 and the mid-1970s a large number of the coaches were lost through neglect and vandalism, and some bad decisions made within the railway organisation.

Many of the 'pairs' coaches, the four-wheel bodies on bogie underframes, were removed from their chassis and dumped around the system without any thought for their historical value. Most of them were left at St.John's, lined up on the centre platform. Their underframes were to be used for the 'Man-tainor' goods services between Douglas and Castletown.

Some coaches were scrapped altogether.

A large number of the more modern (a relative term!) vehicles were lost in a series of fires whilst in store at St.John's carriage shed after the closure of the Peel and Ramsey lines. Natural decay was a problem too, due to the highly changeable weather on the island.

It is only in the last few years, since the construction of two new carriage sheds at Douglas and Port Erin, that every coach can now be stored under cover, especially important during the winter months.

Above left: F46 today. The larger F series were built with full height partitions, with three third class, two first class, and a small luggage/guard compartment. The seats in the guard's compartment, which are often used for passengers, are hinged, designed to accommodate as much luggage as possible.

Left: F10 of 1881 in the new Douglas carriage shed, in the current red and cream livery; it had only just been varnished. To the right is one of the 'Empress' vans, in faded red-brown. The name derives from the year they were constructed, 1886, Queen Victoria's silver jubilee. Two vehicles, F27 and F28, were built for carrying passengers' luggage, either consigned in advance or in connection with the busy boat trains.

Below: F27, one of the 'Empress' vans, in the old carriage shed at Douglas shortly before it was emptied and demolished in 2001. One of the coach underframe runners is in the foreground, whilst a very decayed and unidentified half brake is coupled to the 'Empress' van.
These two vans have carried various liveries - coach red (which soon turned to a salmon pink); purple lake and off-white; and this rather shabby shade of blue with the previous 'pink' showing through.

Below: the other 'Empress' van, F28, is seen outside the carriage shed at St.John's in rather better condition as No.8 Fenella approaches the station with a Ramsey-bound service in the summer of 1956. These vans are of the same body style as the small F series coaches, with wooden frame and body. They have been used for many activities since the decline in the requirement for luggage vans - permanent way, stores, and even ambulance.
Photo: the late David Odabashian.

THE ISLE OF MAN RAILWAY

Liveries

Colour schemes have varied considerably over the years, from green to chocolate brown; purple lake with off white panels, similar to the London and North Western Railway; a two-tone tan and chocolate similar to the Lancashire and Yorkshire Railway; all over deep red; and the well-known post-war red and cream.

The reds and creams have not been constant over the years, partly due to weathering, partly to a different shade of red being used during the 1980s.

A small but significant detail in the application of the post-war red and cream livery is that the two colours were divided by a 1" black line above and below the windows. However, during the 1980s this dividing line was replaced by one of orange. In addition, the wording 'Isle of Man Railway' was applied in the same orange in vinyl-cut lettering to all the coaching stock, replacing the company crest.

Roofs are a difficult subject, as smoke and weathering played a large role. Many started as white or light grey canvas but soon turned to black; some were originally painted black.

Top right: F35, one of two three compartment first/third saloons from 1905 that contained two very plush first class sections. With the addition of corridor connections, F35 is now part of a bar set, but otherwise externally it is nearly as built. The first class sections have been retained in original condition with a through doorway installed, whilst the former third class portion now houses the bar. Seen in May 2003 in the new carriage shed soon after the coach had been varnished.

Right: F75, known as the Governor's Saloon. This is one of the original 'pairs', made up of four-wheel coaches A12 and C9. One was the Governor's Saloon whilst the other was used by the Duke of Sutherland. They were 'paired' in 1926 onto a new Metropolitan underframe. The interiors of this coach are very different from the standard 'pairs'. The seating is around the outside walls of the coach in a U shape between the doors with hardwood folding tables in the centre. In 1967 Lord Ailsa had an opening made between the two compartments.

Right: after the Second World War, a number of vehicles, including many of the 'pairs' coaches, were painted in a brown livery, almost red oxide in colour, which was prone to fade to pink after some time exposed to the Manx weather. 'Pairs' coaches F66, F67, and F74 are seen in the carriage shed at Douglas in 1998 with C1, in red and cream, in the foreground.

Below: a diamond frame coach bogie.

The present situation

I have to admit that despite several visits to areas not normally accessible to the public, I failed to notice the decline in functioning coaches in recent years. Even in view of what occurred in the 1970s, the fleet is well short of the old railway operations.

For that reason, I felt the need to dig into the archives and ask questions to establish details of the current passenger stock. Perhaps I should have known better but to my dismay I did not have to delve too far.

In the railway's heyday there were often trains of fourteen or more coaches; today one could not form one train of that length, as only around a dozen vehicles remain in traffic. Others have been left to rot further since the 1970s cull, while some still exist but in private ownership off the railway.

On the positive side, what is available for travel today represent superb examples of coachbuilding, a tribute to the skilled craftsmen of the Douglas workshops who have kept the stock in service, remembering that not one vehicle is under 100 years old.

There have from time to time been rumours that the Peel line was to be rebuilt, but despite

the welcome availability of motive power at present it would not be practical with the shortage of passenger rolling stock.

Many previous publications have described the full extent of passenger vehicles, their builders, dates, and history. This basic list is principally for the benefit of the would-be 'modern image' Manx modeller.

Serviceable fleet 2006

F9	Brown, Marshalls & Co.	1881
F10	Brown, Marshalls & Co.	1881
F18	Brown, Marshalls & Co.	1894
F26	Metropolitan	1896
F29	Metropolitan	1905
F31	Metropolitan	1905
F39	Bristol & South Wales [1]	1897
F45	Metropolitan	1913
F46	Metropolitan	1913
F47	Metropolitan	1923
F48	Metropolitan	1923
F49	Metropolitan	1926
F54	rebuilt IoMR [2]	2000

[1] former Manx Northern 'Foxdale' coach
[2] former 'pairs' coach scrapped in 1968, used as a container/p.w. runner, original chassis used in rebuild

Above left: typical coupling arrangements - centre 'chopper' buffer couplers, side safety chains, and vacuum brake hoses. The vehicle on the left is fitted with a handbrake - the operating wheel is enclosed in the black semi-circular casing.

Above centre: the brake wheel hatch inside one of the saloon coaches. When locked shut it conveniently prevents any tampering with the brakes.

Above: the simple hand brake handle in the brake end of F39, the Foxdale coach.

Below: the standard wood grain effect compartment partition, and a standard gas lamp housing (now with electric light bulbs).

Below left: an unidentified saloon receives a total rebuild at the back of the carriage workshops in Douglas in 1999.

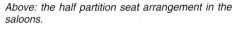

Above: the half partition seat arrangement in the saloons.

Above centre: the typical interior of one of the saloon coaches in present condition. Note the diagonal planking of the floor.

Above right: the first class compartment in one of the large F coaches (F46).

Right: the original style reversible back tram type seating in the third class compartment of F36, with a fixed seat back at the bulkhead. Note the limited leg room.

Surviving passenger vehicles not in running condition

Remaining on railway premises

F15	Brown, Marshalls	1894	derelict, Douglas carriage shed
F21	Metropolitan	1896	repatriated from Ireland awaits restoration in Port Erin carriage shed
F25	Metropolitan	1896	derelict, Port Erin carriage shed
F27	Metropolitan	1897	Empress van, in store on the railway, beyond repair
F28	Metropolitan	1897	Empress van, in store on the railway, beyond repair
F30	Metropolitan	1905	involved in prolonged restoration for many years
F32	Metropolitan	1905	involved in prolonged restoration for many years
F36	Metropolitan	1905	Royal Saloon, on display at Port Erin Museum
F43	Metropolitan	1908	derelict, Douglas carriage shed
F75	Metropolitan	1873/1926	Governor's Saloon, on display Port Erin Museum
N42	Swansea Wagon Co.	1879	(MNR Cleminson) privately owned, awaiting restoration

Off the railway but on the island

F15	Brown, Marshalls	1894	extremely poor condition
F25	Metropolitan	1896	whereabouts and condition unknown
F66	Metropolitan	1873/1920	latter dates refer to the pairing on bogie frames. These three vehicles are the only remains of the
F67	Metropolitan	1873/1922	1920s paired coaches. They were left out in the elements for many years and have consequently
F74	Metropolitan	1873/1921	suffered severe damage. They are stored less their bogies and running boards. It is sad to think that these historic and original 1873 vehicles may never see the railway again.
N41	Swansea Wagon Co.	1879	Manx Northern Cleminson, body only, in poor condition, was used for many years as the mess hut outside Douglas running shed.
N45	Swansea Wagon Co.	1879	Manx Northern Cleminson, privately preserved on the island
C1	Metropolitan	1873	body only; was part of pairs coach F64 of 1912. At the time of writing this coach body rests beside the water tower at Peel. The other half of the pair, B19, was destroyed by a fire. One fears that elements near the River Neb will encourage further deterioration.

Off the island

A number of passenger vehicles were purchased for private preservation and removed from the island during the 1970s and 1980s.
Both the former Manx Northern Railway bogie coaches F37 and F38 have been preserved but the location is not known.
Several steel Metropolitan bogie underframes were sold to the Ffestiniog Railway in the 1970s.
Most of these are now under the new Welsh Highland Railway coaches.

Chapter 13

Freight stock

In narrow gauge terms, the Isle of Man Railway boasted an enormous fleet of freight vehicles. However, a solely freight train was rarely noted.

Open wagon M13 in August 1955.

Open wagon M12 in June 1954.

Open wagon M66 in June 1954.

A dedicated goods train was a rarity on the Isle of Man Railway: on a daily basis, wagons catering for the limited freight business were generally attached to the back of the next passenger train along the line, time being allowed in the passenger timetable for shunting as necessary, although on certain market days a complete train of livestock vehicles was not unknown.

The once vast mineral traffic from Foxdale was worked in separate goods trains.

During the war periods, the wagon fleet was used extensively on war work, carrying such things as spoil from Foxdale and bricks from Glenfaba (Peel), and other supplies for building the RAF and naval air bases at Jurby, Andreas, and Ronaldsway.

To accommodate what freight there was, the railway owned a comprehensive collection of goods stock. Some vehicles were purpose-built by recognised builders on the mainland, while others were made on re-cycled four-wheel coach underframes, and some special vehicles were constructed in the works at Douglas.

Conveyance of goods ceased in 1965. From then on, the remaining collection of freight vehicles that still existed at that time faded away. Some items were sold, but most that were left simply fell apart where they stood, or were cut up and burned by Manx Metals at Ballasalla in the mid-1970s.

Numbering

The numbering system followed on from the coach fleet; as that culminated with the F series, the goods stock started at G. Both the IoMR and MNR had wagons of similar types, so to identify them after the amalgamation, the MNR wagons had a letter R placed after the wagon number. Thus van 'Gr14' was a Swansea-built wagon from the MNR, while a similar IoMR van was simply marked 'G' and then the number.

Current goods stock

Unfortunately what is left is a minute collection, whether original or replica. There is no genuine freight traffic; most items are now only really used for permanent way duties; on occasion they are bodily moved by road to be shared with the Manx Electric Railway.

It is now impossible to see a genuine example of every type of goods vehicle that has run on the IoMR, but replicas of H and M wagons have been built, otherwise examples of these two most widely used designs would not be evident today. Just three original vans still exist.

Below left: open wagon M10 in a siding at St.John's in August 1955.
Four photos: the late David Odabashian.

The wagon types

M

A four-wheel two-plank dropside wagon with slightly higher ends, curved at the top. They were considered the standard wagon, with a 6 ton load capacity. They were designed and built as mineral or ballast wagons but throughout their working lives they were to be seen carrying almost anything, even passengers' luggage. They were even used as storage units by the locomotive department, and could often be seen around Douglas carrying engine parts or a boiler.

They were built by various manufacturers between 1877 and 1926 - Ashbury, Metropolitan, and Swansea. Some were also built by the Manx Northern Railway, so there were many variations in size and detail.

Below: M70 in Douglas carriage workshops. The parts it is carrying belong to No.8 Fenella. This is one of the Metropolitan 1926 batch. Some of the M series were built by the IoMR using the frames from the original four-wheel coaches when they were 'paired'. Three of these wagons were converted by Lord Ailsa to carry oil tanks from road vehicles, in an attempt to increase the freight business.

Right: H9 was one of the original 1873 Metropolitan-built mineral wagons. These vehicles had three-plank sides, whereas the M had two. Designed as mineral wagons, they ended up being used for anything. Some were converted with timber extensions to enable livestock, generally sheep, to be conveyed in them.

Below right: the remains of an H wagon which were used in recent years to build a replica, H1, which was delivered to the island in 2001.

H

This was the wagon which was meant to be the standard but the M series was soon preferred by the staff. The H was introduced from the start in 1873, the first coming from Metropolitan. Only forty-five were built because of the preference for the M. The last was supplied in 1900.

They were of three-plank construction with a centre drop door. Some of them had timber extensions added to enable them to carry smaller livestock such as sheep.

This class of wagon was until recently almost extinct except for the remnants of one that could hardly be described as a wagon, but the Isle of Man Supporters' Association have built a replica, numbered H1.

L

These were bolsters which ran in pairs for carrying timber. L1 and L2 were built and delivered by Metropolitan in 1874; they were 12' long and 6'3" inches wide with a wheelbase of 6'6". Wheels were 2'3" diameter. Six of these vehicles were built, the last two being made out of four-wheel coach chassis by the IoMR around 1910; these two were later (but as far back as 1916) further converted to vans Nos.G17 and G18.

None of these wagons now exist.

Right: originally there were just four of these L wagons built by Metropolitan and designed to carry bulk timber.

Below, left and right: the IoMR has only ever had one purpose-built well wagon. It carried no number or prefix. It was built in Douglas in 1936, and was intended to carry the railway excavator to Foxdale to clear the spoil heaps. It has since, of course, been used for many different tasks, true to IoMR practice. It was eventually replaced with a new vehicle, built in the workshops at Douglas.

A number of other well wagons were created by converting coach chassis in the 1960s, under the Ailsa regime, for container traffic.

G

Vans capable of carrying six tons, on a wheelbase of 8'. Some were built with 'portholes', the idea of which was to make them suitable for carrying livestock.

The first batch was delivered in 1873, and they too were sourced from the usual suppliers. Some G vans were later built by the railway on the original four-wheel coach chassis as the 'pairs' coaches were put together.

A total of nineteen vans were built, of which a few still survive.

Note that some of these vehicles had side planking in various directions and patterns.

During the 1960s a number of G vans were fitted with vacuum brakes and higher mounted couplings so they could be used between the former County Donegal railcars.

K

These vehicles were purely for livestock, although photos exist of some wagons being well overloaded with hay. The original batches, dating back to 1873, were built without roofs, with diagonal outside planking and double side doors.

From 1908 the IoMR built its own livestock wagons on the now usual source of redundant coach chassis; these wagons had vertical outside planking, so it is easy to identify them. Any unroofed vehicle that had survived being scrapped had a roof added after around 1912.

R

These were not designed or purpose-built, but were created in 1967/8 during the Ailsa period by removing the 'pairs' coach bodies to give bogie flat wagons for use on the container service. One of these chassis was rebuilt in an experiment as a well wagon. Like the container service, it failed.

A few of the R runners still exist: some have been converted to ballast hoppers, whilst the remainder have had wooden platforms fitted for permanent way purposes.

An important observation for modellers is that any weight carried makes an interesting bend or dip in the middle of the frames. This was evident in the mid-1960s during the container traffic era.

Fish wagons

These were purpose-built by the IoMR. There was once a busy fishing industry on the island, with herring, mackerel, and kipper processing, especially in Peel. Five of these wagons were built to carry fish products in boxes, baskets, or barrels. They had removable two-plank sides, and a capacity of 3 tons. They were 17'6" long, 5'10" wide, and 1'3" high from floor to the top of the sides. They never had a letter code in the numbering system, simply the words FISH WAGON on the side.

Cranes

Three cranes have been used on the IoMR, although only two are of IoMR origin.

Crane No.1 was a small 5 ton mobile crane, similar to a yard crane, on its own running gear, the frame of former coach A12. It had a wooden jib and was manually operated.

Top: G1, an 1873-built Metropolitan van, stands with G19 at Ballasalla. G19 was built by the IoMR on the frame of a four-wheel coach around 1921. It has been adapted with collapsible platforms for tree cutting, and vacuum braked. It was one of the vans modified to run between the railcars in the 1960s.

Above: Gr11, a former MNR van, at Port Erin in July 1956.   Photo: the late David Odabashian.

Below: K19 and K26 at Ramsey yard in 1953. Cattle wagons originally came from several suppliers - Metropolitan, Ashbury, and Swansea Carriage & Wagon Co. but K10 to K26 were built by the IoMR on spare underframes after the four-wheel coaches were 'paired'. Many of the original batch were delivered without roofs and some remained as such throughout their lives.

Photo: the late David Odabashian.

THE ISLE OF MAN RAILWAY

Above: crane No.2 was saved from the cutting torch at Manx Metals in 1974 by the Isle of Man Railway Society, and is seen here on an isolated section of track at the former Union Mills station on the Peel line.

Above right: crane No.3 at Douglas in front of the Manx Northern Cleminson six-wheel coach body N41 which was used as a mess for many years, now removed.

Crane No.2 was a more substantial piece of equipment, a breakdown crane built and supplied by Richard C.Gibbins & Co. of Birmingham in 1893, mounted on its own running gear.

It too was hand operated and had a lifting capacity of 8 tons. This crane still exists, and is on display at Union Mills station.

Crane No.3 was not of IoMR origin and is in fact a recent 1990s re-incarnation. It is a steam crane with a vertical boiler and started life on Laxey quay on a standard gauge chassis. It was restored privately and now resides and works on the Isle of Man Railway. It is self-sufficient and can propel itself along the track as well as manoeuvring loads mechanically.

Current freight stock

G1	Metropolitan	built 1873	in original condition.
G12	Swansea	built 1873	restored privately and returned to the railway.
G19	IoMR	built 1921	one of a number used between the railcars in the 1960s. It was later modified to carry equipment to cut trees over the line before being placed in store off the railway.
H1	Metropolitan	built 1873	replica built 2000.
M78	Metropolitan	built 1926	replica built 1998 with parts from M70.
Well Wagon	IoMR	built 1936	new wagon built by Douglas workshops in 1999.

R runners (currently carrying original F prefix)

F57	Metropolitan	1873/1919	original pairs, bodies removed 1995.
F62	Metropolitan	1873/1927	original pairs, bodies removed 1968.
F63	Metropolitan	1873/1920	original pairs, bodies removed 1968.
F65	Metropolitan	1873/1910	original pairs, bodies removed 1975, now Douglas-built twin ballast hopper. Often seen on MER.
F70	Metropolitan	1873/1910	original pairs, bodies removed 1975, now Douglas-built twin ballast hopper. Often seen on MER.
F71	Metropolitan	1873/1911	original pairs, bodies removed 1967.
F73	Metropolitan	1873/1920	original pairs, bodies removed 1967.

Above: the former F50 'pairs' underframe was converted to a runner for carrying containers but had been fitted with two-plank side panels in two sections, upon which some wit has chalked 'DOUBLE M'. Pictured at Santon.

Left: the underframe of 'pairs' coach F54 in 1995 in Santon yard, complete with brake wheel, and timber decked throughout the length of the chassis. This runner has since been withdrawn from service and a new replica 'pairs' coach built onto the frame. The vehicle behind is another 'pairs' chassis, from F65, converted into a ballast hopper.

Chapter 14

Liveries

Over the years Manx locomotives and rolling stock have carried various different colour schemes: the modeller concerned with an accurate representation of period needs to determine the details.

Many modellers will know that obtaining the correct colour for rolling stock or structures in proprietary paints is not easy, and sometimes impossible for smaller independent concerns. This generally means mixing colours from the model paints commercially available. With no colour charts as a guide, we find ourselves with a problem from the start - not forgetting that colour representation is always somewhat speculative.

In *An introduction to modelling the Isle of Man Railway*, David Lloyd-Jones has a useful

section on model paint colour suggestions, which I used as the starting point for my own models.

When exhibiting my Isle of Man Railway layout *Port Foxdale* (RAILWAY MODELLER September 2002), I am often asked why the red engines are different shades. The replies I gave never seemed to convince, so I carried out my own research to justify my answers.

I made several paint swatches. For example, for the painting of an engine in the 1967 'Ailsa' green, I produced several paint mix options

and took them to the island and placed them against No.1 *Sutherland* which at that time was still in that livery in the Port Erin museum. This was much better than using photographs, which we all know can lie as far as colour is concerned! The same approach was adopted for the coach liveries.

Later, the staff of the Isle of Man Railway were especially helpful.

The railway went through a period of painting its fleet in historic liveries. These were achieved by taking samples by rubbing down paintwork on rolling stock layer by layer to find and re-create the correct shade. For example, two locomotives were rubbed down in this way between 1980 and 1991, *Kissack* and *G.H.Wood*, to determine the original 1873 livery: two very different shades of what was expected to be Brunswick green were found.

This would have been a result of the pigments and mixtures used at the time of initial painting, whether at the locomotive or rolling stock builders or in the Douglas workshops.

Top: during the final decade of the Isle of Man Railway Company Limited, the serviceable fleet was still painted in the 'Ailsa' apple green. No.10, No.4, and No.12 are seen in 1973 in Douglas yard, in what was the last corporate livery of the railway company.

Left: restored to working order in 1998, No.1 Sutherland *is seen in green outside Douglas running shed. However, this darker apple green is far from the 1967 'Ailsa' green, which was nearer to NER green, and neither approximate to the original dark green.*

Right: 1980 saw the introduction of 'historic' liveries. Rubbings were taken from each locomotive to give as accurate a reproduction as possible of the original livery. No.10 G.H.Wood (seen outside Douglas shed) was painted in the 1873 livery of Brunswick green with vermilion-black-vermilion lining but with certain 'modern' alterations - the footsteps would have been black originally. The green running gear would also have been painted black after the First World War.

Below right: after a number of years running in this scheme, it was decided that the loco looked very drab, so it was repainted in the 1873 green but given yellow-black-yellow lining. The loco is seen outside Port Erin engine shed in 1998.

At the time, paints were made from earth, carbon, mineral and inorganic (chemical) sources. It was possible to produce a wide range of colours, so it is not surprising that the most common colours for locomotives were green, red, or brown (with apologies to the Great Eastern and Caledonian railways!). There was a price implication, as some pigments cost considerably more than others.

The history of paint mixing is not appropriate here, but some extremely interesting facts came out of my research which do have a bearing on the finish of locos and stock. Paint would have been mixed at the time of use in the workshops. The dry powdered colour pigments were added to a wet mixture of shellac, red lead, linseed oil, turpentine, and drying agents. Only a slight measure too much or too little of the pigment powder would make all the difference to the finish. The light in which it was mixed would also affect the colour as the painter gauged the result. The paint was then varnished. Varnish was produced with kauri gum, rosin, boiled linseed oil, benzine, and real turpentine: again the proportions could affect the finish, not to mention the number of coats applied. As a result of this paint mixing, and the varnishing, plus weathering and cleaning over the years, it becomes an interesting task to reproduce accurately any company's period livery.

The introduction of modern paints changed all this. Today, the railway uses synthetic paints so the whole fleet matches. I understand that each coach is varnished annually to prevent colour change and weathering problems.

It should be noted that with the exception of 1945/6 and 2001, the changes in the liveries of IoMR locomotives and coaching stock did not coincide.

Locomotives

In 1873, the three original engines were delivered in a dark Brunswick green. All subsequent engines up to No.16 *Mannin* in 1926 were supplied in this livery. Lining was applied to all locos in vermilion-black-vermilion. This was carried through and after the Second World War, despite the proposed introduction of a new Indian red livery from 1945/6.

Right: No.9 Douglas, out of service for many years in Port Erin shed, was given a coat of paint supposedly in the historic Brunswick green livery with vermilion-black-vermilion lining. It was later found that the green paint used had been left over from the recently redecorated exterior of Port Erin station!

By adding small amounts of yellow or black to the base colour, the modeller can re-create the probable differing shades for each loco.

Repaints would have been few and far between, so over time the Manx weather will have made quite a difference and faded the colour. Patch painting was common, even into the 1970s. This makes for a quite an impact on the finish of any model.

Initially the driving wheels, cylinder covers, and pony truck axlebox covers were also green. However, in later years all the running gear was in black.

It is also worth noting that during the two world wars some engines appeared without lining, when and if any painting was done.

The Manx Northern Railway originally had a very ornate livery of Tuscan red (including the wheels) with vermilion-black-vermilion lining, and some extremely elaborate gold-leaf embellishments to the tank sides, with the railway's insignia, although No.3 *Thornhill* (later IoMR No.14) was lined out in a similar fashion to the IoMR engines.

It was decided in 1945/6 to revitalise the railway and give it a new image. However, repairs were desperately needed to the entire fleet of rolling stock so this was to be a slow transition. Paintwork would have generally been in a poor condition.

The new livery for the locomotives was to be Indian red with yellow-black-yellow lining. Cylinders, pony truck axlebox covers, and driving wheels were also red, and lined. Coupling and connecting rods were painted red or white.

The differing reds for the base coat are easy enough to represent in model form by using the colours in the chart.

1965/6 was a turning point in the company's history. It was thought that the railway had closed its doors for good. However, in 1967 the Marquis of Ailsa leased the line, giving the railway new life.

The new livery for the locomotives is believed to have originated in an idea presented by the late Reverend Teddy Boston. The few locos that were still serviceable at this time were painted in an attractive apple green with white-black-white lining. As previously, elements of the running gear were in the body colour. The colour was similar to LNER Doncaster green and was the same throughout the fleet. Known as 'Ailsa' green, this was to prove the last corporate image of the Isle of Man Railway Company. In model terms this is not an 'off-the-shelf' green and much mixing and testing is required. At the time of writing, only No.5 *Mona* is still in this livery, although very faded, rusted, and hidden away.

Top left: the early 1980s brought the return to red of one loco, No.11 Maitland. *However, this was not the post-war Indian red. An orangey red/brown was chosen. A small detail worth noting is that the loco lost the brass safety valve cover at this time.*

Middle: No.15 Caledonia *in the replica Manx Northern red livery, taking water from a temporary water tower at Port Erin in 1996.*

Left: No.11 Maitland *outside Port Erin shed in the current Indian red livery.*

THE ISLE OF MAN RAILWAY

With this change of management, some redundant locomotives were put on display at St.John's and subsequently in Douglas station. Some were painted in the new green. However, No.14 *Thornhill* was painted in a dark red similar to the old MNR red, but lined out as the IoMR engines. It was not the Indian red of the IoMR.

In 1968, No.15 *Caledonia* was withdrawn and put on display painted in a dark red with MNR lining and number to simulate the former company's livery, but again it was not actually the MNR Tuscan red.

During the 1980s/1990s under Manx government ownership the working fleet, still small in number, was painted in different historic liveries. However, it is true to say that some were far from authentic and resulted in what the railway authorities came to describe as photogenic liveries. No.12 *Hutchinson* is a prime example - it carried a royal blue livery for some years; attractive enough, but with no historical justification. No.15 *Caledonia* was later painted in a similar but darker livery.

On the appointment of a new Director of Public Transport for the Isle of Man in 2000 there was a welcome return to the Indian red and post-war coach livery.

But modellers must beware as there are variations between these well-meaning imitations and the original livery.

In the original post-war Indian red, the cab footsteps were all black; the current version has red and yellow lining, and black steps.

No.4 *Loch* retains the Manx Northern style 'three legs' and the numeral on the buffer beam, a legacy of the 1990s schemes.

No.12 *Hutchinson* has lost the numbers on the cab side.

The markings on the cab rear vary, while the Isle of Man Railway Company crest has not always been applied to the tank sides throughout the company's history.

The signwriter's art spread across many aspects of the system - locos, coaches, freight stock, and buildings. Many items were not repainted for years, and whilst rolling stock liveries might have changed the old styles would have lingered in places alongside the new.

This page shows some locomotive bunker sheet numbering. Although the typeface is the same, the positioning varied. The line under the 'o' was sometimes wavy. The position of the lining itself on the back sheet also varied. The numbers are painted cream with black shading, not white and black as the lining.

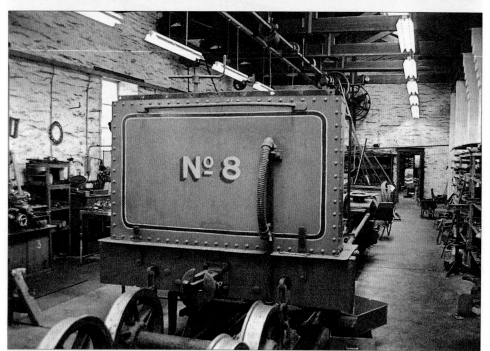

Below: the two liveries apparent in the early 1970s on the redundant locos at Douglas. All the lining was hand painted on both the older Indian red and apple green livery. The red livery was on No.3 Pender and the apple green is No.16 Mannin.

The loco illustrated within the company crest transfer is No.16 Mannin, depicted in the pre-Second World War dark green livery.

Note that the crest was not applied to locos when the Indian red livery was used between 1944 and 1967.

Even when laid on its side and set aside, as in the view above, the essential elegance of the slender Beyer,Peacock copper-capped chimney fitted to the Manx locos cannot be disguised. The practice of fitting metal numerals to the chimney sides aided identification.

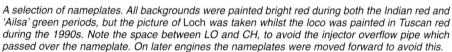

A selection of nameplates. All backgrounds were painted bright red during both the Indian red and 'Ailsa' green periods, but the picture of Loch was taken whilst the loco was painted in Tuscan red during the 1990s. Note the space between LO and CH, to avoid the injector overflow pipe which passed over the nameplate. On later engines the nameplates were moved forward to avoid this.

Left: part of a collection of reference samples for the railway signwriter in the carriage and wagon workshops, Douglas. Traditional hand-painted signwriting methods are still very much in use today. During the 1980s orange vinyl lettering was used on the coach fleet, and did nothing for the appearance, being quite out of character.

Suggested colours and sources - a paint guide for modellers
Part 1: Locomotives *(see p.102 for notes on coach liveries)*

Manx Northern up to 1905
Carmine Red, Humbrol 174.

Isle of Man Railway

First livery, 1873 onwards
Brunswick Green, Humbrol 3 (produced only in gloss finish) or 105; Revell equivalent 62. Add matt yellow or black to allow for pigment changes in mixing differences.

Lining - initially vermilion-black-white, later vermilion-black-vermilion.
Running gear, driving wheels, cylinders, pony truck axlebox covers- originally green and lined, later all black.
Coupling and connecting rods were at this time unpainted.
No fleet number on the rear bunker sheet.
Some engines appeared unlined during austerity/wartime periods.

After World War Two, Indian red.
For an ex-works (1945/6) finish - Humbrol 100 Red Brown, Revell equivalent 33 Red; for an older and weathered look - Humbrol 180 Dark Red.
(Mix the two to create the differing pigment shades.)
Running gear - as main body colour.
Pony truck axlebox covers - Indian red, fully lined.
Lining - yellow-black-yellow.
Coupling and connecting rods were painted white.
All locomotives carried number on rear of coal bunker, painted in cream with black shading. This is continued to this day.
(Note that 1873 green persisted due to repairs to rolling stock and locomotives being deferred after the war effort.)

'Ailsa' Green 1967
Railmatch LNER Doncaster Green
    mixed with Bright Lemon Yellow and a hint of White.
Lining - white, black, white.
Running gear - as previously.

Pony truck axlebox covers - green, fully lined.
The connecting rods were painted bright red, later (from 1970) white.
1968/9 display livery for No.14 was as No.15 - Phoenix Precision Paints Co.Donegal Red, with orange-black-orange lining. Coupling rods - Red.

1980s – 1990s
The 'historic' liveries applied in this period were carried out using modern synthetic paints.
Several engines, including No.10 G.H.Wood, were rubbed down layer by layer until the original 1873 livery was found.
The paint selected as the closest match was 'Tekaloid' Middle Brunswick Green. The nearest Humbrol colour is 3.

Present day
In 2002/3 the steam fleet was returned to Indian Red (Dulux ref.6040Y90R).
The nearest model colour is Revell SM 331.
Coupling rods - currently dull silver paint on all locos.
The exception is No.15 Caledonia, in Royal Blue (Humbrol 15 or Revell 54).

Notes
No.1 Sutherland was returned to service in 1998 in an 'Ailsa' green lookalike livery.

No.5 Mona is the only locomotive still in true 'Ailsa' green livery.

In 1968 No.15 Caledonia was painted in a lookalike MNR red for use on a special train, with standard red coupling rods, vermilion-black-vermilion lining on the tank sides only, and cream shaded black 'M.N.R.' lettering. The nearest model colour is Precision Paints P883 Co.Donegal Loco Red. Caledonia remained in this livery until 1993/4 despite being withdrawn during 1969.

Diesel loco No.17 Viking was first (1992) painted in the 'Tekaloid' Middle Brunswick Green (Humbrol 3). In 2003 it was repainted in a totally different Apple Green, officially 'Thorpe Green' by Masons Paints. The nearest Humbrol colour is 38 Lime Green, Revell equivalent SM364.

original green

Indian red

new Indian red

'Ailsa' green

Tekaloid green

Thorpe green

Above: No.15 Caledonia, seen here in 1995 on Snaefell in the replica Manx Northern livery.

Above and below: the latest acquisition, Hunslet diesel No.18 Ailsa, is still in the contractor's white livery but has been adorned with a cast nameplate and shaded numbers.

Below: in 1992 new arrival No.17 Viking entered service in the 1873 Brunswick green with vermilion-black-vermilion lining. The red running gear was retained from its German livery.

Above: No.12 Hutchinson in current Indian red livery at Port Erin.

Wagons

Generally, wagons were all painted a light grey with black or dark grey metal fittings and underframe. Apparently, the MNR simply used creosote on the plain timber for some of their vehicles.

Lettering was in white, shaded black in the early days.

The cranes were in a red oxide, very similar to that used on the ironwork of bridges, etc.

It is fair to say that the wagons were not repainted on a regular basis and in later years many appeared in what was no more than bare weathered wood with rusting ironwork.

Right: M78 and Gr12 at Douglas in 1999. The M is the recent replica built by the Isle of Man Steam Railway Supporters Association, whilst Gr12 (as the prefix r denotes) is an original MNR van. These vans varied in small details depending on the builders - Metropolitan, Ashbury, Swansea, or the IoMR. The main differences are in the size, the pattern of boarding, and the ventilation arrangements.

Paint guide for modellers *Part 2: Rolling stock*

Manx Northern Railway

Initial livery
Grained teak, Humbrol 110 Natural Wood or Humbrol 84 Matt Mid Stone.

1894 onwards
Purple Lake and Off-White, a mixture of Humbrol 68 (gloss) + 85 Coal Black, and Revell White; apply varnish to yellow the panels.

Isle of Man Railway

1876 to 1916/7
Precision Paints GWR Chocolate, and Revell White; apply varnish to yellow the panels. (Revell White, being less brilliant than Humbrol lends itself better to the off-white required.)

1917 to 1945
Above waistline, Humbrol 62 Matt Leather, Revell equivalent 85;
Below waistline, Humbrol 98 Chocolate; no Revell equivalent.

Mid 1920s onwards
New stock was delivered and painted in a similar fashion to the final Manx Northern Railway livery, Purple Lake and Off-White. Older stock appeared repainted in this livery over a period of time. It is very likely many Tan and Brown vehicles existed until after the Second World War.
First appearance, although short-lived, of the company crest on coaches.

First and second world wars
During these austerity years, stock could be painted in any colour that was in the workshop - generally any shade of brown. This did not constitute an official railway livery.
Humbrol 98 Chocolate or 160 Brown; no Revell equivalent.

Post war 1945/6
Precision Paints Post Office Red or Humbrol 60; no Revell equivalent. (The two options allow for different age and weathering.)
Railmatch British Rail Cream and Railmatch British Rail Red (Early) or British Rail Crimson.
(Again, two options offered depending on age and weathering required.)
The second noted in each case can also be used for the 1980s livery.
The BR Crimson can be used for the all-red saloons.
The older bogie coaches which had panels down over the solebars had a black frame painted onto the base of these panels to enable the livery to 'flow' along the rakes.

Post war, later years
Humbrol 73 Matt Wine; no Revell equivalent.
Some coaches, particularly the 'Pairs', remained in this livery until the end of their working life.

1990s
Mixture of Humbrol 68 + Coal Black 85 for the main colour, with Revell White for the panels.
'Empress' Vans - Humbrol 73 or Humbrol 98.

Freight wagons
Railmatch LMS Wagon Grey, with white or black added to modify the shade to represent pigment variations or weathering. Ironwork in black.

Cranes - Halfords Plastic Primer, Oxide Red; or Revell 73.

Coaches

With limited evidence, the livery of the early four-wheel coaching stock is very speculative. It is believed that some were painted green and white and some chocolate brown. There is not really sufficient information to make accurate suggestions as to which model paints should be used.

Around 1875 the IoMR ordered its first bogie coaches. These were painted with off-white upper panels and chocolate brown beading and panels below the waistline. It is believed that the four-wheeled stock was repainted in the same livery around this time.

The MNR stock was absorbed in 1905 into the IoMR fleet: all carried a purple lake and off-white livery. Research suggests that the MNR vehicles were not repainted until 1917 when all coaches on the IoMR were painted in a two tone tan and brown livery, similar to the Lancashire & Yorkshire Railway. During this period coaches delivered new were painted in off-white (varnished white) and purple lake. These coaches all carried the IoMR company crest on the sides.

After the Second World War, coaches appeared in a red and cream livery that was retained until around 1980. This livery had red below window level and again at cantrail height, with a cream band at window level.

Right: in the red and cream livery, the 1905 saloons were given the full treatment, carrying the initials on the body side with the fleet number below, as on these vehicles the cantrail above the windows was not deep enough. Lettering, with no serifs, was painted in cream with white, green, and blue shading. These vehicles look very grand in this livery.

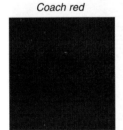 

Coach red *Coach cream*

1886 to 1916/7 purple & ivory

1917 to 1945 brown & tan

post-WW2 red & cream

post-WW2 all-red/brown

Right and below: coach signwriting on the IoMR has been very consistent throughout its history in terms of font and style, the major changes being to the main colour, and the shading where applied. These examples illustrate the main signage on the current livery and as used post-1947. Fleet numbers are usually on the cantrail, between the top of the windows and the roof line; class designations are carried on the appropriate doors, below the waist line. The main body colours are separated by thin black lining.

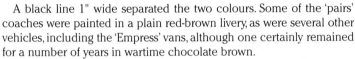

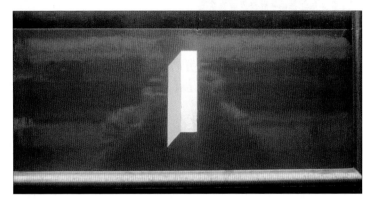

A black line 1" wide separated the two colours. Some of the 'pairs' coaches were painted in a plain red-brown livery, as were several other vehicles, including the 'Empress' vans, although one certainly remained for a number of years in wartime chocolate brown.

In 1974, the saloons were painted all over coach red. It was not unknown around this time to see rakes of coaches in two shades of red and cream and all red.

The 1980s and 1990s saw many changes.

The railcars and then some of the saloon coaches were painted with white upper panels and bright red lower panels, the livery of the bus company. The rest of the coach fleet retained the red and cream livery although slightly darker than the 1940s version, and with yellow/orange vinyl lining and lettering, as used on modern road vehicles, on the sides of the coaches - a tasteless effort to advertise Isle of Man Railways, as it was known then.

By the mid-1990s all the coaching stock had been painted in the old MNR livery of off-white upper panels with purple lake beading and lower panels.

Some stock, for example the existing 'pairs' coaches and at least one of the 'Empress' vans, still carry the all red-brown 1940s livery, although very faded. Fortunately this survival did enable me to match the colour.

Ageing and weathering

We may ignore the differences between the old lead-based hand-mixed and the newer synthetic paints, for the simple reason that the diverse weather patterns on the island have a profound effect on the longevity of any colour and surface finish.

The purple lake took a very short time to darken almost to a black, whilst the varnished off-white turned to a buttermilk. This occurred even on the 1990s version of the livery.

The early 1940s wartime red-brown vehicles turned to a pale patchy salmon pink but this would then remain stable for years. This includes any grounded vehicles such as the Cleminson outside Douglas shed.

In the mid-1940s, with the introduction of the now famous red and cream, both the initial pigmented mixtures and the subsequent synthetic coatings remained stable for longer. The earlier paints darkened with age whilst the current livery is varnished each year, creating a similar effect. However, even the varnishing did not prevent the eventual 'pinking' of the red and darkening of the cream; brake dust and smut deposits no doubt also played a part.

Despite the turntable being installed at St.John's specifically in order to turn coaches to alleviate uneven weathering, this task was rarely carried out. The consequence was that after a period of time any rake of coaches would be a slightly different shade on the 'sea' side to the inland face. This was the case on both the north and south lines as the sea was on the same side of the train for the entire route, the left-hand side heading away from Douglas.

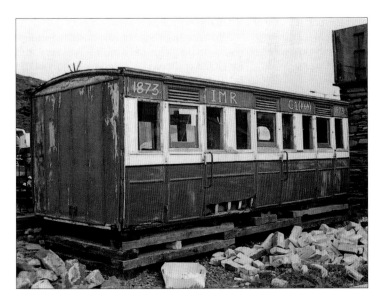

Left: C1, one of the original four-wheel bodies subsequently 'paired', next to the Peel water tower in 2001. It still wears the 1945/6 red and cream livery, although badly weathered.

Chapter 15
Modelling

Having studied the real thing, this concluding section looks at what can be achieved as a result of spending that little bit longer on the research.

I do not profess to be a particularly skilled modeller, but research makes all the difference. The use of more than one source of information is essential, and studying the real thing first hand is a bonus. We are fortunate in the case of the Isle of Man Railway, as although much has gone or been changed, plenty of the original infrastructure still exists.

Track plans or station layouts have been published for most if not all of the IoMR stations: some have even shown changes over time. Such plans are good for planting the seed modellers need to get going, but may be lacking when we come to the matter of how much space is available and the need to scale down the prototype.

Not all the IoMR station layouts are straight - Union Mills on the Peel line and Port Soderick on the south line come to mind. So you can be creative and think of ways to work within the limitations of the space that is available.

In 4mm scale, most IoMR stations would need a passing loop in the region of 6' long to allow the crossing of trains that in their heyday could have been up to fourteen bogie coaches plus the loco. Clearly, most modellers will need to shorten the trains to bring the length of the proposed station within practical limits.

The aim is to make an interesting layout with plenty of scenic atmosphere (however that is defined) and operation as near to prototype as possible.

Douglas would be a great subject, with the different architecture, and a wealth of loco and train movements, especially at the end of day when the loco crews put everything away, but the layout would need to be pretty large. Because of the sheer size of the site, I have never taken the time to measure and scale just how much space would be needed to model the Douglas terminus as it was before the 1980s downgrading. But I know someone who has ....

St.John's too, would make a good layout, with the splitting of Peel and Ramsey trains at the Douglas end of the station and the Foxdale branch sweeping around that vast curved embankment and back over the main line. Imagine operating St.John's on Tynwald Day! Not to mention the unofficial races that took place when the two trains simultaneously made their way north and west respectively. But it would need plenty of space.

The viaducts at Glen Mooar and Glen Wyllin were magnificent structures, each slightly different in terms of ironwork, but with the same style of stonework.

Glen Mooar viaduct would make a very striking layout centrepiece, but from the glen floor to the top of the centre piers, the underside of the girders, is 75' or 300mm in 4mm scale. The viaduct consisted of three 60' lattice girders, which would be 720mm from one side of the glen to the other just to the end stonework. With some additional landscape it would make a superb model but would need a lot of area and depth - a dimension too rarely considered in layout planning. To give the true impression of the height of these viaducts, even if modelled exactly to scale, careful consideration would have to be given to the viewing point or eye line.

Glen Wyllin, which was slightly lower, had the amusement park below and Kirk Michael station just yards away to the north, so these could be combined to make a very interesting diorama.

There is not a station on the whole system that could not be modelled, one way or another, and still be given the Manx atmosphere, whether replicated to the nearest millimetre or adapted in size.

Architecturally, there are many different styles of station building, from the Manx Northern Railway double gabled Peel red sandstone buildings to the simple wooden shed Class Three buildings such as at Kirk Braddan. Crosby and St.John's were similar buildings, of a Norwegian style built in wood; they have superb matchboard exteriors. They would all be relatively simple to construct from plasticard.

The track itself is a matter of individual choice. Peco now produce 12mm gauge track with flexible yard lengths, turnouts, including some very nice curved points, and a diamond crossing. (In passing, it should be noted that only one of these existed on the system, in the sidings at Foxdale.)

Although the Peco track is designed to represent metre gauge in HOm, it serves very well for OOn3. It should be noted that many of the IoMR turnouts of Y formation and these are not commercially available. However, the 3mm Society is a source for these.

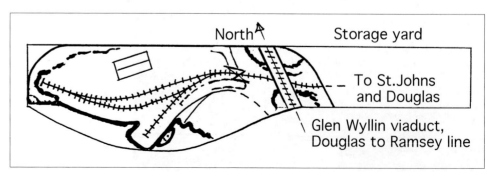

Right: IoMR No.15 crossing Glen Wyllin viaduct high above Port Foxdale with a northbound train to Ramsey.
Photo: Len Weal, Peco Studio.

More experienced modellers might wish to build their own track.

Rails were always spiked to the sleepers, except at Gob-y-Deigan on the Ramsey line which was chaired to stop the gauge spreading, and also on the Foxdale branch. Soldering rail to printed circuit board sleepers would represent the spiked track quite well, although in the early years the Isle of Man Railway used half-round sleepers with flat sections cut out to take the rail - this is more of a challenge! The Manx Northern Railway used conventional square cut sleepers from the outset.

The modeller in 4mm scale is now quite well served with much stock available in kit form. Any of the steam locomotives can be built from kits, for almost any period, with the potential to add extra detail. A good selection of coaches and wagons is also available in kit form, but there is also plenty of stock that is not produced commercially which would be relatively easy to adapt or scratchbuild.

For me, the most difficult choice is which period to model. The railway has had such a diverse and chequered history, and each period has its own merits.

From modeller's inspiration to inspired model

Because of space limitations, my layout could only be 5' long by 18" wide at most, so there was no way it was going to be a prototypical model of any of the IoMR stations. As already mentioned, the passing loops at any of the stations are of such a length that made it impossible to think of a prototype.

On such a small stage, the scenic setting was therefore going to play a large part in conveying an authentic impression not just of the railway but also the Manx atmosphere.

The scale was to be 4mm to the foot, the track gauge 12mm - OOn3.

Port Foxdale

Armed with my many photographs taken in the early 1970s, I started a layout. I promised my wife that it would be a model of the prototype Foxdale terminus on a small coffee table, complete with spoil heaps and a scale 1 in 49 gradient to a fiddle yard.

Here I made the big mistake. Do not believe that working in narrow gauge you need less space. I did not scale the plan and laid the Peco track following the real layout on a plain baseboard. Suffice to say it did not fit the coffee table! *Port Foxdale* is therefore my second attempt at an IOMR layout, having learned the hard way!

Maps of the Isle of Man from the early years of railway development between 1884 and 1888 show a proposed railway from Peel in the west and St.John's to Kirk Michael. This proposal, if it had gone ahead, would have provided a second route north to Ramsey.

Opened in August 1886, the real Foxdale Railway was built to transport the products of the lead, zinc, and silver mines in and around Foxdale. The railway, some two and a half miles in length, had a rising gradient throughout of 1 in 49 from St.John's to Foxdale and the mines. Once built, this line was leased to the Manx Northern Railway who operated trains from the outset.

Unfortunately the mines' fortunes were short-lived and they failed around 1900. This failure and other financial restraints, plus competition from other concerns on the island, led to the Manx Northern being incorporated into the Isle of Man Railway in 1905.

If we assume that the 1884 proposed line had been built as an extension to the real Foxdale branch, it would have arrived at a junction on the west coast of the island somewhere near Kirk Michael. 'Port Foxdale' would have been the terminus at the sea end of Glen Wyllin, just below the viaduct that carries the St.John's to Ramsey line. A quay would have been built as an alternative transfer point to Ramsey, to handle shipments of products from the mines. Trains serve Port Foxdale from that junction, from St.John's including Foxdale, and from Ramsey and Kirk Michael.

I set the time of the layout around what is known as the 'Ailsa' period for two reasons.

First, my initial holiday on the island in 1964 left a lasting memory of when all these fine Beyer, Peacock locomotives were painted in a wonderful shade of Indian red with red and cream coaches.

Second, from the 'Ailsa' period through to the 1970s the locomotive fleet was painted in an apple green, introduced in 1967, and this has turned out to be my favourite livery. I wanted to use both colour schemes.

Left: Port Foxdale station building, a copy of the prototype Foxdale terminus. It is made on a card base and frame with plasticard walling. The slates are individual pieces of watercolour paper. Chimney pots are whitemetal castings and match the originals well. It is important to not over-do the weathering on a model but slate roofs do seem to need a lot of attention. The red brick walls have a yellow decorative brick row right through the middle and the corners - not easy to get right in this scale.
Photo: Len Weal, Peco Studio.

Above: on the tower roof at Douglas station there was, in the railway's heyday, the legend I.O.M.RAILWAY in big whitewashed letters. In the early 1970s the legend was restored with a 'Victorian' lady added. I could not resist it!

Below left: the stop block, from Port Erin. The prototype was removed in 2005, making this an historic representation.

Below: the grounded coach body used as a mess is a former Manx Northern Railway Cleminson, inspired by the example that sat outside Douglas workshops for so many years. It is built from a brass kit, placed on a plaster 'concrete' base. Many coats of paint with different techniques were used to get the right weathered finish.

Baseboards

These are quite simply built with two frames of 50mm x 25mm timber, 5'3" long by 18" at its widest, with a curved front formed of hardboard added; they were fixed together one on top of the other to create a single baseboard. This dual level gave the depth for the quay and the water. The lower frame, which was to have no track, was then covered in chipboard to give a firm surface and base; the top frame was covered in soft fibreboard to allow the required track fixings and access holes, etc.

Track and track layout

This was simply going to be a home layout to run my favourite Manx engines and rolling stock, my own three-dimensional picture postcard. Vast amounts of operating line were not going to be required, just an end-to-end section of track attached to a fiddle yard. It had to include a run-round loop vastly shorter than any of the prototypes, and a siding onto a pier - and be electrically very, very simple!

Peco HOm 12mm gauge track was used, laid to allow for as much of a typical IoMR station atmosphere as possible. Once fitted with point motors and micro-switches, the track was ballasted and buried IoMR-style using carefully washed beach sand to near enough Manx station ground colour.

Pointwork within station areas was always kept clear of whatever mineral was used for ballast, and the ground around and within was nearly always black with oil deposits. This practice was followed on the model.

The single running line follows roughly the course of the stream that actually flows the length of Glen Wyllin.

Buildings

It was important to gain an overall Manx feel to the model, so the emphasis was on putting together prototype structures that had character and were relevant to either the IoMR or MNR. I had already started making the station building for the Foxdale terminus for the first

attempted layout. This was to be finished to form the basis of the design, using the real geographical setting of Glen Wyllin, just south of Kirk Michael. The station building and water tower are direct scale copies of the prototypes at Foxdale. They were built in card covered

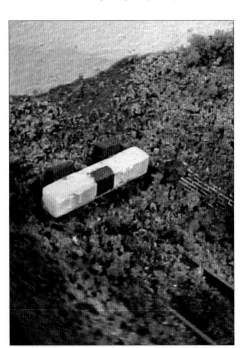

with embossed plasticard, with watercolour paper individual roof tiles, and whitemetal castings for details such as the chimney cowls, guttering, and seagulls. As the layout was to reflect my memories of the 1960/1970s the station roof was adorned with the white-washed sign that was originally to be seen on the tower at Douglas station advertising the 'Victorian Steam Railway'.

Great care was need in painting the yellow brick quoins on the walls, otherwise a straight row of detailed decorative brickwork was going to look awful.

The water tower was built in the same way as the station building. The water tank was made out of a mist bottle lid, and has been modelled with the same worrying lean as the prototype at Foxdale. The water within the tub is plasticine; this allowed a ripple effect which was then painted black and varnished.

Enormous poster boards were placed at the side of the track, as at many of the IOMR stations, generally to hide something from the railway traveller, as at Crosby where there was a siding used for manure! These were made from off-cuts of rail for the vertical supports, plasticard matchboarding, and many hours at the computer producing the posters.

As No.16 Mannin *arrives at Port Foxdale, No.1* Sutherland *brings a goods train over the Glen Wyllin viaduct. The piers were clad with air-drying clay and scribed whilst the girders and decking are all plastic extrusions.*
Photo: Len Weal, Peco Studio.

Below: Foxdale water tower. The water 'tub' is a plastic bottle lid covered in rust powder and then filled with varnish. For those who remember the prototype, note the tub has the same lean as the real thing.

Below centre: the Port Foxdale starter, a Manx Northern Railway signal and post. The single lens and frame have rusted away, as has the lamp housing, leaving only part of the wooden 'fish tail' signal arm. This was a copy of the Ramsey home signal, although modelled a little shorter.

Below right: Stevens & Son locking ground frame. There were two of these on the IoMR, one at St.John's and the other at Foxdale. Like all the signal equipment, it would have been out of use at Port Foxdale by the 1960s-1970s.

The harbour is loosely based on the inner curved quay at Port St.Mary. The base of the wall is formed by edge of the upper baseboard, faced with embossed plasticard stonework, with balsa wood bargeboards suitably weathered. The top concrete surface is decorator's filler with sand mixed in and lightly painted.

The small lighthouse is a copy of the original Victorian and now replaced cast iron 'mustard pot' lighthouse on Peel east quay.

The boat started life as a really cheap and very nasty looking souvenir, bought from a seaside shop just for the nicely-shaped solid wooden hull. Once carved out, the hull was given a new rudder, propeller, and a rusty coat of paint below the water line.

These pictures, taken from the sea, show the harbour and the lighthouse.

The curved quay was inspired by the inner harbour at Port St.Mary and the palm trees, although not the right species, are like those which can be found virtually anywhere on the island.

The boat is not a copy of a Manx fisher, more a Clyde puffer. It started life as a cheap seaside souvenir fishing boat, well worth the price for the wonderful shaped solid wooden hull. All the nasty bits down to the deck were removed, as was the coat of gloss blue paint, the hull was carved out, and a new deck and fittings constructed out of plasticard. 'PL' is the shipping register code for Peel; the number - well, it was my birthday when I finished it; and that is in the month of May, so the boat is called MEAY, Manx Gaelic for May.
Photos: Len Weal, Peco Studio.

Above deck level, all was scratchbuilt out of plasticard, following numerous photos of Clyde 'Puffers'. Fishing nets are made from black tights.

The boat was given a Manx Gaelic name and a Peel registration number.

The water is of the hot resin type, poured on to a thick layer of budgie grit and sand. This caused some very anxious moments! The resin was either not hot enough to flow or too hot, which had an extremely unhealthy effect on the plastic sea walls. For a low tide appearance, the finish of the water looks reasonable. Do not let anyone tell you it does not scratch or crack, because it does - very easily. It also looked too clear, despite adding a small amount of green to the grit.

I subsequently coated the cast resin with a high gloss varnish which has helped the look a lot.

Seaweed is coarse scenic material with many coats of gloss varnish.

The sand on the beach is a natural Manx mineral, from Douglas beach.

A Manx Northern Railway Cleminson six-wheel coach body forms the very run-down mess room, sitting on a cast concrete base. The prototype for this was until recent years outside Douglas running shed, painted a very weather-worn green. More recent research has shown that outbuildings such as these would have been a red oxide during the modelled period, but it took so long to distress this vehicle to its present condition with broken boarded-up windows and rough peeling paint, etc., that I am not about to change it!

I had to include some palm trees on the station, which always raises comments about the authenticity of them actually growing on the Isle of Man. Palms really do grow all over the island, the best known on stations are at Santon and Sulby Glen. These examples are from a kit, and although not the correct variety of palm, they were the most convincing ones available. Some doctoring was required to lose the plastic moulded look!

There are only two signals on the layout - strictly speaking there should not be any! In keeping with the tradition of the old IoMR company to mix, match, recycle and re-site, I have included a (scratchbuilt) original 1873 IoMR slotted home copied from one at Mill Road, Castletown, and a MNR 'fish tail' starter, which would once have had a single red spectacle; both are modelled out of use.

I wanted to include some red sandstone cliffs, which so dominate the Peel coastline, although this is not quite right for the cliffs at Glen Wyllin, which are of yellow sandstone. The cliffs and landscaping are made from polystyrene, foamboard, and cork, with plaster and decorator's filler detailing.

Left: No.1 Sutherland *shunts on the quay with a spoil train from the mines at Foxdale made up of two M wagons. By the 1970s the freight stock remaining was in a poor condition, with soft rotten wood frames and very rusty ironwork. I have been careful to try to recreate this appearance for some of the wagons.*

Manx enthusiasts who knew the Foxdale station site would remember the leaning water tower container; the same lean is depicted on this model building.

Track is Peco HOm, with real sand as ballast. It was necessary to wash this well to remove any salt so as not to corrode any electrical contacts and the surface of the rails.

The level crossing gates are copies of those at Kirk Michael, with the addition of a replacement post on one corner. Originally crossing gates had very robust square posts, rounded off at the top. As they rotted and eventually required replacing, posts constructed from old rail were used, three rails strapped together in the form of a triangle with bracket hinges welded in place.

The tunnel to the fiddle yard at the rear is a replica of the river bridge at the top end of Glen Wyllin.

Right: memories of Peel beach in the summer sunshine. 0-6-0T No.15 Caledonia *arrives on a local branch train.* Photo: author.

Far right: the view of Port Foxdale station from the viaduct. No.16 Mannin *is ready to leave with a mixed train.*

Photos: Len Weal, Peco Studio (unless noted).

The ground foliage was several coats and shades of rough grass. A Manx cliff-top would not be complete without a covering of the wonderful magenta heather and yellow gorse which give something of a unique atmosphere.

The part viaduct is a copy of the Glen Wyllin viaduct, although it is placed a little further down the glen and nearer the sea than the prototype. The sandstone piers were made from air-drying clay wrapped around a shaped foamboard inner. Care had to be taken not to allow it to dry too quickly, to prevent shrinkage. This enabled the stone detailing to be carved at a leisurely pace. The girders, slightly shallower than the prototype, are constructed using plastic profiles and balsa wood.

Right: No.5 Mona *and coach F44 ready to depart.*

Below: No.16 Mannin *arriving with a first class saloon.*

Below right: No.1 Sutherland *on the viaduct.*

Locomotives and rolling stock

Locomotives are all built from the basic Gem or Branchlines body kit with Branchlines chassis. The Branchlines detailing kits were used: these offer the different style brass domes, pop valves, steam pipe castings, and pipe wires needed to produce a locomotive from almost any period from 1873. Other details are down to the individual.

All the locos are lined by hand, a task that is very time consuming, but well worth it.

The IoMR locos, despite some having been rebuilt several times over the years, show great respect to their original design and builders' Gorton heritage. For this reason, it was very difficult to refrain from finishing them all in ex-works condition. However, to give some historical and operational authenticity, some locos have been weathered. No.16 *Mannin* was by 1964 in her last operating season, in a very poor state mechanically and cosmetically. This has been reflected in the finish of the model.

No.15 *Caledonia*, the only engine not from Beyer, Peacock but built by Dübs of Glasgow for the MNR, was originally modelled in smart ex-works condition in the very short-lived 'Ailsa' green livery she carried on the day of the re-opening in 1967.

No.1 Sutherland

Top right: the Gem body kit and the Branchlines chassis and detailing kit. At the start it does not really matter which of the IoMR Beyer, Peacocks you are modelling. However, from the stage pictured it is important to look at photos of the specific prototype you require, for so many features vary, such as boiler size, chimney type, smokebox detail, pipework, tank patches, cab spectacles, handrails, lamp brackets, etc., etc. This kit will eventually be turned out as No.13 Kissack in Indian red.

Right: No.16 Mannin, another Gem body and Branchlines chassis. Body detail is almost complete, with the hand-painted lining well under way. If I were to build this kit again, I would replace the cab roof with brass sheet, as the cast whitemetal version supplied is rather thick.

Right: No.15 Caledonia. *I never saw this engine run in this short-lived livery, which I think suits it better than any other. The special event shield and flags were made in an evening; computer clip art came in handy for the flags. The white headcode discs are plasticard put through a hole punch. This was the headcode all the locomotives carried on the re-opening day in 1967. Red oval special train boards are also simply cut from plasticard.*

Below and opposite: No.1 Sutherland *and No.5* Mona *in the liveries of the 1960s and 1970s. Note the differing pipe work and other details. Both of these engines have been weathered very heavily, and the brass work has been left to tarnish. The IoMR fleet was not always kept in ex-works condition even though the loco crews took a lot of pride in their workplace. The engines went for some years without repainting, and with generous cleaning with oily rags, plus the island's natural weathering, it did not take long for the colour to change appearance. It was also not unknown for a patch to be welded or rivetted on as a repair, and just the patch would be painted as new.*

No.5 Mona

Left: the question of colour is a very emotive subject. How do you get the right colour when you are miles away from the prototype and years on from the finish you require? Further, for most of the railway's history the paint was mixed as required for each locomotive or coach, so they were not precisely consistent and all exhibit different shades anyway! Then there is the effect of exposure to light and weather .... especially noticeable with the Indian red.

Photographs too, original or published, can display many variations, as a result of processing, printing, and reproduction, not to mention fading with age.

Then there is the matter of the lighting conditions when the prototype was observed, and under which the model is to be painted, and then viewed. Quite apart from any consideration of any differences in how individuals physically perceive colour ....

So I spent an evening mixing up different shades, recording the mixes, and applying them to sample sheets. I then took the sample sheets to the Isle of Man and tested them against the real thing, because the real thing cannot lie! I cannot relate what my wife thought of this exercise, but it did work to my satisfaction.

Left: No.1 Sutherland was the first IoMR loco model I built, and slightly modified. The small snowploughs, back and front, are made from thick watercolour paper, soaked, wrapped around a pencil, left to dry all night, and then cut to shape. The cab wind sheets are also made from watercolour paper. This loco is heavily weathered as the prototype was out of service by the period modelled.

Below: No.5 Mona, built using a Gem body kit plus a Branchlines chassis and detailing kit. Tank patches were added using very thin brass sheet with rivets punched out. Lamp brackets have been fitted to allow for the addition of removable lamps and assorted signs such as this 'Special Train Following' board. The lining, as on all my locos, is all hand painted by brush.

Initial stock - motive power

No.1 *Sutherland* Branchlines kit.
No.5 *Mona* Gem body, Branchlines chassis.
No.13 *Kissack* Gem body, Branchlines chassis.
No.15 *Caledonia* Branchlines kit.
No.16 *Mannin* Gem body, Branchlines chassis.
Nos.19/20 ex-CDR railcars, modified Anbrico body kit now with custom-built chassis.

Since completing the layout, several additions have been made to the locomotive fleet - No.2 *Derby*, No.4 *Loch*, No.7 *Tynwald*, No.8 *Fenella*, No.9 *Douglas*, No.10 *G.H.Wood*, No.12 *Hutchinson*, and No.14 *Thornhill*, plus Manx Northern No.2 *Northern*, the 'might have been' 2–4-2T rebuild, and a bogie diesel from the West Clare (even though negotiations to purchase them came to nothing). I have also modelled the Wickham trolley from Ramsey pier that came to the railway for a brief period, and the 'new' Schöma diesel No.17 *Viking*.

Left: a revised and improved version of No.5 Mona. Not doing full research in the first place led to the model needing to be altered.

I had wrongly fitted the large type of displacement lubricators on the smokebox sides. These were removed and a new mechanical lubricator made from a small square block of plastic, a small brass wheel, and brass strip, all joined to copper wires leading back to the smokebox.

Ornate front lamps have been fitted to suit the 1970s 'Victorian Steam Railway' period.

Those who model smaller independent railways know that finding transfers for the crests and lettering for locos and rolling stock can be difficult if not impossible. The IoMR started putting the company crest on its loco fleet in 1967 when the 'Ailsa' green livery appeared. These are reproduced on my locos using a computer printing onto thin paper, and fixed with varnish.

The original finish was drab, too drab for a loco in service, so the paintwork was cleaned and an oily varnish has been applied.

Right: No.15 Caledonia, *modelled in near ex-works condition, in what was, as it turned out for the prototype, a very short-lived livery. Painted 'Ailsa' green in 1967 for the railway's re-opening, it would not have had time to get too dirty or weathered as it was soon repainted into the Manx Northern Railway red livery.*

After a number of failures on passenger duties, it was withdrawn from service.

Right: No.16 Mannin *modelled and finished depicting its last season in service. It was withdrawn in 1964 after some forty years with the same 3'6" diameter boiler. Many photos show this loco in its last season in a very poor shabby state. Not being a great lover of ex-works condition models and considering the period being modelled, it would not have been right to have it looking pristine.*

Below: No.13 Kissack. *A certain amount of modeller's licence has been used in building this model as in the period the layout covers Kissack would certainly not have been in ex-works condition Indian red but would have been in 'Ailsa' green. It did enable me to model the extra pipework all the locos had during the 1950s and early 1960s, and the brass safety valve cover (which is now on* Maitland). Kissack *was a common sight during the 1970s, one of the few engines that kept the railway running, so I had to build her.*

Note that locos which have mechanical lubricators do not carry the large brass smokebox lubricators seen here on Kissack. *They had a simple connector and pipe running down the smokebox side to the running board and the lubricator.*

The weather sheets on the cab sides are made from painted very crumpled absorbent paper. I generally use a thin watercolour paper as it has a good texture and is very flexible for rolling up to the cab roof or tucking in between the handrails.

A satin varnish is used for ex-works condition engines - do not use gloss, it is far to shiny and unrealistic. To obtain that oily polish sheen engines have after a while in service, a mixture of Ronseal satin and Humbrol matt varnish is used with a hint of track colour. Smokebox and running boards are Humbrol 'Coal Black'. Brass and pipework is kept polished on this loco with a fibreglass brush.

Left and below: two views of the completed body of No.2 Derby.

Bottom left: No.7 Tynwald. The loco is not strictly appropriate for the period I model as by then it had been dismantled. The model is in unlined Brunswick green, much weathered.

Bottom right: No.8 Fenella.

No.2 Derby

For No.2 *Derby* I took one of the Branchlines kits for the smaller Beyer, Peacocks and reconstructed the whole thing to the state in which the engine was delivered to Douglas in 1873. The green of that period is a replica of the hue that was found on No.13 *Kissack* when rubbed down in the 1980s. Lining is the 1873 vermilion - black - white. All that remains to build is the chassis.

No.7 Tynwald

The model was completely scratchbuilt from styrene sheet and represents how the prototype can be seen on the island today.

I wanted to experiment with paint textures. I well remember among the display of redundant locomotives in Douglas in the early 1970s was one with a very pitted surface on the boiler (I believe it was No.14 *Thornhill*). I found that weathering powders did not achieve this. Peeling paint was also a challenge. So modeller's licence was invoked to build a locomotive that had not seen the inside of the paint shop for a number of years. This was often the case on the IoMR so the experiment was not completely implausible.

My choice was No.7 *Tynwald*. It was the first of the Isle of Man locomotives to be broken up (in 1945; the only other one was No.2 *Derby*, in 1949) generally due to worn out parts, lack of spares, and lack of funds. The collision with No.10 *G.H. Wood* in 1928 may also have played

a part in the decision. So I was going to take this locomotive past its dismantling date.

Livery was the next choice. So as not to take the locomotive too far past historical accuracy, it was initially finished in ex-works condition, in Second World War unlined Brunswick green with black running gear.

Weathering was carried out in the normal places, such as where the steam hits the pony truck, with blackening of the paint work, oil-covered smokebox, cab roof, tarnished pipework .... but how to peel and pit the paint? After some experimentation a sharp scalpel was used to prick the paintwork out and a stencil brush to stipple partly dried matt varnish. It worked a treat.

No.8 Fenella

No.8 *Fenella* was inspired by Alan Catlow who built his model from part of a Gem kit plus a scratchbuilt boiler. No.8 *Fenella* has some significant details that need alteration or the provision of additional parts if a kit is used as basis. In 1937 it was fitted with what was called a 'Special' 2'10¾" boiler with twin Ross 'pop' valves and a vertical fronted welded smokebox. It was the only 'small' Beyer, Peacock to have this feature, giving it a distinctive appearance. This boiler was carried by the engine until it was withdrawn. (Boiler sizes are quoted without lagging and sheeting.) By the late 1960s it was also the only small Peacock still in service, so very suitable for *Port Foxdale*.

Above and right: No.9 Douglas, *notable for the Salter safety valves and split buffer beam.*

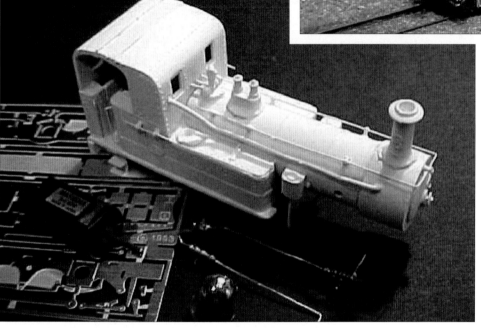

No.9 Douglas

I have generally endeavoured to paint the locomotives in the last colour used between 1960 and 1970, with a small amount of modeller's licence as some had been withdrawn before 1960. No.9 *Douglas* is a good example: withdrawn in November 1953, the prototype was seen to carry the 'Ailsa' green livery in the 1970s as one of the redundant locos on display, so the model is not stretching the point too far. One of my aims with the layout was to provide myself with a 'picture postcard' of what I remember and loved so much about the railway. One of the things that sticks in my mind is seeing No.9 *Douglas* parked in the Port Erin departure platform at Douglas.

No.9 is the only small Beyer, Peacock left on the island in almost as delivered condition. A mass of pipework and split buffer beams were therefore essential. The splits were produced with careful use of a circular saw. As the only remaining loco today which has Salter safety valves on the boiler, it makes for quite an interesting diversion from the many other differences between the fleet. The safety valves were extremely fiddly and frustrating to fit!

Without knowing the true dimensions of the finished boiler on this engine, some guesswork was involved for the model. I have to say that looking at the remodelled boiler and photographs of the prototype, there seems little difference in appearance to the other 'small' engines except for the smokebox.

A standard kit for a 'small' Beyer, Peacock kit was used, the whitemetal boiler castings being glued together and shaved slightly to try and give a visible difference in diameter. The smokebox supplied in the kit was converted with car body filler to produce the straight fronted version. The whole smokebox was sanded down and the cast rivets removed at the same time.

The twin Ross 'pop' valve cover was cast using a mould, made from wrapping Blu-Tak around a cast part on another engine. This was then filled with car body filler, left to harden, and rubbed down. Safety valves were taken from the spares box.

Other pipework was added as per photographs of the period, with all the normal Beyer, Peacock fittings.

Tank patches were made from shim brass with rivets pushed out with a bradawl. Builder's plates were added at an early stage as they are painted in the body colour.

The cab rear sheet had the spectacles opened out to rectangular, as per the prototype.

The loco looks splendid painted in the 'Ailsa' green it carried for just three seasons, from reopening in 1967 to 1969 when it was withdrawn with a boiler failure.

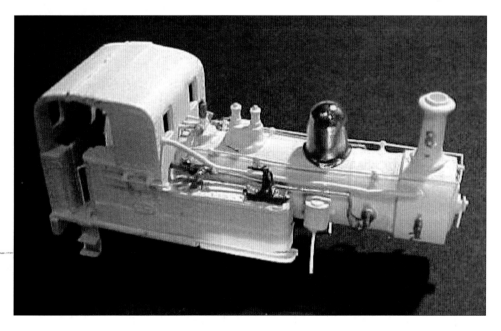

No.10 G.H.Wood

No.10 *G.H.Wood*, once known as the Secretary's locomotive, has a very warm and vivid memory from my youth. It was not only one of the five stalwart engines that kept the shortened Isle of Man Railway running in the late 1960s and 1970s but one that I shall never forget as it was the very locomotive upon which I was able to ride on the footplate, while it was working a permanent way train, almost unheard of by that time. It was meant to be the first locomotive built for the layout but turned out to be the last, but it will always remind me of that experience. It is worth noting the tank patches on this engine as no other had this pattern, an upward curving plate at the front and cab end of the water tank - just one of the many ways one could identify locomotives without seeing the chimney or rear sheet number or nameplate.

No.12 Hutchinson

This is the last of the large of the Beyer,Peacocks I shall probably build! It was ever-present in the 1970s and I have fond memories of it. I have to say it was not an easy model to make as by the time I got round to it Gem had changed the castings for the body, which needed many alterations to fit it to the chassis.

I have made the tank numerals too big but this is not a feature I shall lose sleep over.

No.14 Thornhill

Thornhill was originally a Manx Northern Railway locomotive, their No.3, built side by side with IoMR No.7 *Tynwald* at the Gorton Foundry in 1880.

For this model I have used the tried and tested Isle of Man Railway practice of recycling and rebuilding to put another locomotive into service. I had made *Tynwald* purely for the purpose of building one of the two dismantled locomotives so I could have something in the old Brunswick green livery. This was fine and enjoyable but too far away from the period of *Port Foxdale*. So *Tynwald* was stripped and rebuilt using a small number of additional and replacement parts. Suitably repainted to the 1946 Indian red it has joined the running fleet.

MNR No.2 Northern

Why would I want to build a locomotive which ran on a railway that was absorbed into the IoMR 1905 and never lived to see service during the period I am modelling, 1960 to 1970? I have, like so many, followed the path of trying to recreate the prototype as accurately as possible, found the pitfalls, and made mistakes. We can set a period and get each rivet in place but take the whole thing far too seriously and not enjoy it or have fun. This project was all about fun!

By 1905 the Isle of Man Railway was made up of not one but three concerns: the original Isle of Man Railway, the Manx Northern Railway, and the Foxdale Railway, which had

Above: No.10 G.H.Wood.

Right: No.14 Thornhill.

Below : No.12 Hutchinson.

been operated by the MNR. The MNR had its own collection of rolling stock with its own individual character, though very few items lasted to the present day.

The aim was to model Manx Northern Railway No.2 *Northern*, one of two 2-4-0 side tank engines built by Sharp,Stewart in 1879 as the line's initial motive power. No.1, virtually the same, was named *Ramsey*. A lower price was no doubt the reason for choosing the builder in preference to Beyer,Peacock.

Both were absorbed into the IoMR fleet in 1905 along with the Beyer,Peacock 2-4-0T No.3 (IoMR No.14) *Thornhill* and of course the Dübs 0-6-0T No.4 (IoMR No.15) *Caledonia*.

The two Sharp,Stewart engines, for various reasons, had relatively short working careers with the IoMR, who appear to have taken an immediate dislike to them. Both were cut up, though not until 1923 and 1912 respectively.

So, where to start? To my knowledge this design of Sharp,Stewart locomotive is not available in kit form in any scale. There were 4mm scale kits by Golden Arrow for the Southwold 'Sharpies', but even though they were also 3' gauge, rare for an English narrow gauge railway, they were much smaller and so not suitable for conversion.

I had no joy trying to persuade possible manufacturers to produce a kit, and no faith in my ability to scratchbuild. The gloom came to an end when Richard Glover of the Greenwich & District Narrow Gauge Railway Society presented me with a very old unbuilt K's 4mm scale whitemetal kit of a Sharp,Stewart engine. This looked ideal for conversion, so out came

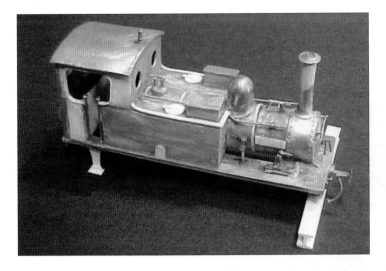

Above: the body of Manx Northern No.2 Northern, showing how the old whitemetal kit was adapted.

Right: the finished model. The loco has quite a different character to the Beyer,Peacocks.

the books, photographs, and drawings to research the fine detail. The *Manx Northern Railway* book by the Hendrys was invaluable.

Although parts were not interchangeable, the MNR 2-4-0T locos had many similar dimensions as the IoMR Beyer,Peacocks, having been ordered on the basis of similar specifications: these were most apparent below the footplate, with cylinders, driving wheel size, driving wheel centres, and coupling rods. However, in place of the Bissel pony truck with 2' diameter wheels, the 'Sharpies' had a radial leading truck with a 2'9" spoked wheel placed behind the slide valve gear.

A Branchlines IoMR Beyer,Peacock chassis was converted to fit the model.

Cutting discs, modelling knives, and the usual tools were passed across the castings to convert the body to a recognisable MNR 'Sharpie'. Some significant alterations were needed, along with the addition of parts from the spares box and scratchbuilt styrene or brass accessories. I have to admit that a great deal of car body filler was used to create some of the mouldings, including the extended tapered chimney. It was this that gave the most concern as the few photographs available show several differences between the two engines, so I made the one I liked! I have also added vacuum pipes to bring it up to date. The most noticeable addition is the MNR No.2 number plate on the tank, which was removed in 1905 by the IoMR: I have put it back!

It is far too interesting a locomotive to stand idle on a shelf. This lead to a difficult decision as to the livery. Should I paint it in MNR Tuscan red, lined out, or use modeller's licence and claim it was retained in traffic until the 1960s? If so, in which livery? I think 'Ailsa' green might be pushing it too far! *Caledonia*, the only surviving MNR locomotive in use in 1968, had been painted in unlined Indian red in 1964, so *Northern* was similarly treated: it suited the 'Sharpie' well.

However, I was not really satisfied with either of these locos in this livery, and decided to repaint them both into the 1969 'Ailsa'

version of the MNR livery, with lining, as it was in this colour scheme that I remembered first seeing *Caledonia* at Douglas around 1970. My colour swatches suggested the finish was very close to Co.Donegal geranium red.

Northern was actually allocated the number 18 in the IoMR fleet, but it was never carried even though its MNR number plates were removed so 18 could be placed on the bunker.

Modernisation – the 2-4-2T proposal

It would be fair to admit when I look back at the *Port Foxdale* project I was a bit of a purist as far as what stock would be modelled. However, this does not have to be the case for anyone who enjoys a little freelance work within the confines of the railway's history.

Modernisation was considered by Messrs. Sheard and Jackson in the late 1940s after the British forces left the island and it was transformed back from an internment camp to the holiday destination so popular prior to the war. Beyer,Peacock were asked to quote for larger locomotives to cope with the expected influx of holiday traffic, and avoid the need to stop for water on the long Ramsey run. Beyer,Peacock's quotations for a large 2-6-2T were rejected as too large

and powerful, as well as not being acceptable to the IoMR budget; instead, responding to a suggestion from the railway, they drew up a design to convert Nos.10, 11, 12, 13 and 16 with extended frames carrying a rear bunker and additional tank, supported by a radial truck.

This fairly easy conversion from a Gem *Mannin* body and Branchlines chassis shows what they would have looked like, but I am pleased it never happened. Then neither did the influx of new holidaymakers - they were enticed to foreign shores, and the idea of modernisation was shelved for another ten years or so whilst the decline of the railway continued.

The railcars, with No.20 leading. The units are articulated between the cab and passenger compartments. Working parts had to be made that were more practical than those supplied in the Anbrico kit. The cast white-metal corridor connections were removed and new compartment ends and folding corridor connections made and fitted. Smaller spoked wheels were fitted to the rear bogies, and underframe fittings were made from scratch, with reference to drawings and photos.

Left: the railcar set with No.19 leading. Note the differences between the units in the windows (cab and side), and in the style of lining on the ends.

Railcars Nos.19 & 20

I dearly wanted models of the two former County Donegal railcars, Nos.19 and 20, as they are quite suitable for the period I have chosen to model, and would add variety compared to the steam locos.

I felt that scratchbuilding such complex shapes was not an option for me. Anbrico had produced a whitemetal kit for these units back in the 1960s. Although long out of production, the kits can sometimes be found secondhand. Following the appearance of *Port Foxdale* at Expo Narrow Gauge in 2001, I was able to obtain a couple of unbuilt kits from fellow members of the 009 Society.

The kit made up into a model that was extremely heavy (around 600 grammes the pair) and difficult to get rolling. It also needed a lot of modification and detailing to produce a realistic model of the prototypes, especially as far as the articulation of the chassis was concerned. The units are articulated between the cab and passenger compartments, and these working

parts had to be made more practical, and the cast whitemetal corridor connections removed. New compartment ends and folded paper corridor connections were made and fitted.

Ignoring everybody's advice, I naïvely thought that fitting a Mashima can motor and gearbox to the front axles of each railcar was going to move them: how wrong I was!

Very disappointed, I left them on the shelf for some weeks, just looking at them, forlornly waiting for some kind of inspiration.

I was then shown a 12mm gauge self-contained power bogie by the Austrian firm Halling which was intended for trams: it would possibly have worked but would have needed a lot of modification, as the prototype's power bogies have coupling rods linking the driving wheels. I would also have to undo all the re-modelling involved in the articulation and change the specially made driver's cab and coach end sheeting with its new flexible corridor connections.

Then I found a photograph taken in 1965 at Castletown showing a G van (G19) sandwiched between the railcars: it was used on occasions to carry passenger luggage or small goods. This was the answer! I could use a G van kit from Branchlines with a Halling bogie. These units have a variable wheelbase which gives the modeller a great deal of scope.

The van kit was built with all the running gear fitted, but less wheels and bearings. The integral roof was cut away from the cast resin body to allow access.

Motor retaining brackets were made from brass and glued in with Araldite. The motor was then installed with the axles moved and matched to the wagon running gear. A false interior platform was made within the wagon, above the motor, to enable as much weight as possible to be added for traction. A new plastic planked roof was fitted, with toilet tissue for the torn canvas roof. The wagon was then painted, weathered, and false chopper couplings fixed

Above: the Halling tram motor unit, which gives very smooth slow running. Similar products come from several sources and manufacturers, in a choice of gauges, some with adjustable wheelbase.

Opposite page, bottom left: the modified Branchlines G van. Note the vacuum brake, which was fitted only to vehicles that worked between the railcars. The higher couplings can also be seen. G19 was not the only van so fitted.

Opposite page, bottom right: press studs soldered to a piece of firm wire are used to couple all three vehicles - an old-fashioned method of coupling, but useful in difficult curved layout situations.

Above: the former County Donegal Railways railcars leave Port Foxdale with van G19 sandwiched between them. The drive was at this time in the G van. The red flag attached to the rear of No.20 is one of those practices only the IoMR could get away with. In Robert Robotham's 'Isle of Man Classic Steam' there is a photo of the railcars at Union Mills that shows this makeshift rear signal 'light'. It just had to be included on the model.

to the higher than normal position to match the railcars. The actual link is effected with press studs.

The two railcars were coupled to the van, back to back, placed on the track, power applied and - it slipped like skates on an ice rink. Despair! I could not believe that all that power was not moving the railcars. It was not physically possible to add any more weight to the van to improve adhesion. The only thing to do was to create more traction on the wheels themselves, perhaps by adding traction tyres.

The wheels have quite a fine profile and anything too thick would throw the wagon out of alignment, and make the flanges useless. Elastic bands were too thick, rubber masking paint did not stay put, carborundum paper was too thick and inflexible. Then I thought of cutting slices from surgical synthetic rubber gloves, stuck on with super glue. The material was found to be thin enough to fit around the wheels without impairing the flange. These gloves come with a 'non-stick' powder inside, so they were washed, dried, and cut open to make a flat piece of material. The two sides have very different surfaces, one matt and one quite glossy. I stuck the glossy side to the tread of the wheel with double-sided tape, avoiding the flange. How long this would last remained to be seen, but at least it enabled the railcars to move, and the remedy can be replicated if required. However, in the exhibition environment this still caused problems, so it was not the final answer.

I eventually had two power bogies made, compensated, complete with the prototypical coupling rods. They were beautifully built by David Woodcock and I could not have asked for a better solution.

A far more convenient way of modelling the railcars now would be the Worsley Works 'scratch aid' etched brass kit. As supplied this requires a drive unit, although some chassis components are included.

Mike Chinery offers a custom 12mm gauge chassis building service and has developed a unit which suits the Worsley Works kit.

Locomotive No.21

By 1960 the Isle of Man Railway was virtually on its knees, and in Ireland the 3' gauge had suffered very badly as well: the railway-owned bus company and the private car were winning.

A move to modernise was partly fulfilled by the purchase of the County Donegal railcars Nos.19 and 20.

Further acquisitions from Ireland were attempted in the form of the three Walker Bros bogie diesels from the West Clare (CIE). For a number of reasons the purchase failed; if they had arrived one wonders how the railway would look today, and if certain steam locomotives would still exist!

History does not prevent us from modelling what could have been and Worsley Works

produce a 'scratch-aid' fret to build the body of these locomotives. Much work has to be done to turn this into a finished model; mine has two whitemetal power bogies supplied by Mike Chinery.

Based on the principle that the IoMR would probably not have spent time or money in 1961 repainting the loco from West Clare green to Indian Red on arrival, I assumed its first Isle of Man Railway applied livery would have been the 1967 'Ailsa' green, completed with the usual painted coupling rods, white-black-white modern lining, and a chevron on the radiators to match the railcars.

Subsequently I repainted the model into Indian red.

This loco will in time be given a name, following Manx tradition: ideas such as Sheard, Jackson, Clucas, or Vignoles, all ancestors or representatives connected to the original railway company.

This was an interesting project, a major contrast to the Beyer, Peacock locomotives, and it has created much interest at exhibitions.

No.17 *Viking*

Photographs and drawings were sent to Allen Doherty of Worsley Works who produced the etchings required for a basic 4mm scale kit in his 'scratch aid' series. Drawings and photographs are essential to complete the kit, although the etchings could be put together without much more research. However, the details not included in the kit will need some homework and time. With these 'scratch aid' kits you do not get instructions, wheels, motor, handrails and all the other essential details that make a finished model of the prototype. All that is up to you, which I think adds to the enjoyment of building the kits.

Worsley have made etchings for me before and they have always been of good quality, but this set for No.17 *Viking* has been designed and etched beyond expectation. The design has been very well thought out, with half etched lines on each side of the fret for folding, and details such as the ventilation grilles and footstep grips. The engine housing needs a crease in the centre of the roof panel and rolled tops on the side panels; all have been neatly etched both sides for ease of bending.

One note of interest is that the simple chassis sides with no spacers could very well be gauged for use on OO9 as well as OOn3.

If, like me, you are no wizard when it comes to electrical items or building motorising units, time should be spent considering how you will power the locomotive before too much construction takes place, especially as far as the chassis is concerned. The wheelbase of 29mm is not too much of a problem but with only 15.5mm clearance within the engine housing it might be! My solution was to install a ready motorised unit, of which more anon.

The first soldering task is to fit all the add-on ventilation grilles which I must admit I thought twice about fitting. Etched grilles exist on the engine housing already, including the radiator cover. However, the overlays were added in case the bases were lost in painting.

The reinforced coupling plates which were added by Isle of Man Railways to the original buffer beams were also applied. These were wafer thin so solder paint was used.

Once fixed in place and cleaned, the next stage is to do the only serious bending required on the whole loco, the engine housing. This has been neatly designed with etched marks on both sides, detail outside and inside for folding and rolling. I prepared myself with cocktail sticks and other tools for the tight outer corners but in the event the whole thing rolled and folded in all the right directions on its own without difficulty.

Soldering and positioning the engine housing to the cab was made easy by an etched grove provided in the cab front plate. I found fitting the radiator sheeting and grille more difficult as the pitch at the top of the etch was not the same as the pitch on the engine housing: I expecting it was a fault in the bending or folding. Having checked all was fine, a fillet of solder was added and filed away smooth.

The cab footplate is lower than the running boards and this requires the complete running board and footplate part to be folded next, and the angle reinforced by soldering. It is very obvious which end is which, but it is essential to ensure the footstep cutout is at the front of the engine and the fold done the right direction.

An adequate cutout for the motor is provided and it is not critical to open or cut this to any other size or shape at this stage.

The other three sides to form the cab are next, but as the rear cab plate also forms one of the two large buffer beams, I decided to work on this area whilst it was flat on the bench. The front beam was also done at the same time. Chain hooks and cowcatchers (which were not fun to solder due to the very fine triangular braces) come as part of the kit, as do the shaped metal cab window visors.

The pipes for the vacuum brakes which were fitted by the IoMR were added at this point from my spares box.

The temptation to fit couplings at this stage was resisted just in case of any slight measurement problems with the height.

To ensure that the engine housing and cab sit in the correct position, it is necessary at this point to fix the front buffer beam to the running board, as the radiator grille must be flush with the buffer beam, almost to the extent that only a fine join is seen between the radiator and buffer beam. This in turn gives the correct position for the engine housing and cab front.

The engine housing cannot be soldered on the inside and quite a time was spent carefully carrying out this task so as not to destroy any etch lines or the fine grilles. A word of warning here: the opening in the footplate for the motor is marginally wider than the engine housing, so a fillet of solder had to be put in the gap.

The footboards can now be folded and soldered into position.

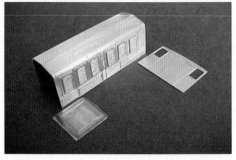

Above: the folded engine housing, which was much easier to do than expected - the fine etched lines made it very simple - with the addition of a line of solder to fix it in place.

Below: the rear cab sheet and both buffer beams were worked on before being soldered to the main assembly.

Below: the completed engine compartment and radiator. A fillet of solder was needed to fill a small gap at the top of the front of the radiator panel.

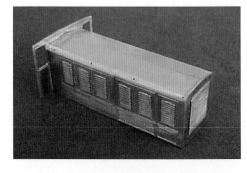

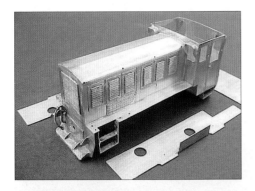

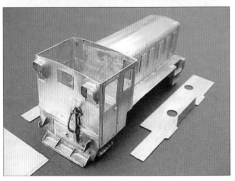

Above: the completed 'scratch aid' kit as supplied - the rest is up to the modeller to complete and detail. The cab roof will not be attached until after painting and fitting glazing.

The plain etched pieces by the body are all that is provided for the chassis - the folded 'shelf' is to support the brake reservoir cylinders.

The cab is very straightforward; drilling out the handrail holes before construction is advisable. As the cab has an integral floor, the roof, once rolled to shape, is not glued on until after glazing and any required cab details are fitted. It is definitely worth pointing out that the fold lines on the roof are to roll the edges down and not up. There are no drip strips on this roof!

The simple chassis consisting only of side plates cannot be fitted until the motor and gearbox has been chosen, measured, and assembled. Spacers will have to be made to suit your requirements.

Note the two 'flaps' on the chassis side plates need to be folded outward to hold the half round brake reservoir tanks; they are not meant to fold inward to support the motor.

Wheel centres have been etched at 29mm and the holes can be further opened up to take bearings if required.

So as far as the 'scratch aid' kit is concerned, that is it! The task now is to complete the motorising so the chassis can be finished. I am certainly not qualified to give any compulsory instructions for this as everybody will have their own ideas. For my model I have chosen a self-contained motorised bogie. Here a problem was encountered because of the limited width of just 15.5mm inside the body shell. Many powered units are made for standard gauge models and I indebted to Andrew Mullins (Branchlines) and Dave Hammersley (Roxey Mouldings) for their advice; however, Mike Chinery came up trumps with a unit to fit No.17. The chassis was then built around this power unit and attached to the body.

The top handrail holes have been etched as on the drawing I received from Isle of Man Railways; this originated from the manufacturers, Schöma, in Germany. In fact, as the loco runs now it is incorrect - it should have six brackets, not four, so a certain amount of filling and drilling has to take place.

Since 1992, a number of other details have changed, including livery, removal of the plastic window and door wraps, oil filler, and the second small vacuum cylinder on the nearside.

To be added are the tool box, axleboxes and dampers, brake reservoir cylinders (three in 1992, two by 2003), sandboxes, lamps back and front, cab handrails, engine roof vents, exhausts, couplings, coupling chains, and - last but not least - builder's plates and nameplates. The prototype plates are aluminium, so brass - as used for the rest of the IoMR fleet - is out of the question. Trying to find someone who could etch these at moderate cost became a project on its own! The nameplates were eventually produced at late stage in the project, again etched by Allen Doherty.

The spares box always comes in handy for these 'scratch aid' kits, and many items left over from other models might find a use. The long toolbox was constructed out of two loco tool boxes left over from a Branchlines Beyer, Peacock tank. The exhausts were carved from whitemetal roof vents from the Roxey Cleminson coach, and the lamps out of wheel bearings. Many details were simply constructed from styrene sheet.

Livery

In building this model I put myself in a situation where the loco is out of period for my layout (1960 to 1970), with steam locos in either Indian red or 'Ailsa' green, so it was difficult to decide on the livery. Bearing in mind that a diesel was considered as far back as the 1940s, I was tempted to paint it Indian red, but that would be far too un-prototypical as this loco was not built until 1958. So as it arrived or as it is were the only two viable choices.

I found the 1992 Brunswick green very drab. If you do wish to reproduce this livery, I think Humbrol no.3 is the best option; it can be used straight from the pot. Lining should be vermilion-black-vermilion.

In May 2003 the loco was in 'Thorpe' green which is available from professional paint suppliers but is very expensive, and there were no small sample pots on offer! This colour purports to be the same as the 'Ailsa' green, but having discussed the subject with the railway's then Director, we decided it was definitely darker, and far from the apple green of the late Teddy Boston's model which seems to have started the light green livery.

So the 2003 green it had to be for my model. All the green locos on *Port Foxdale* were painted in a colour obtained by matching against No.1 *Sutherland* whilst it was still in the Port Erin museum during the 1980s. This was not going to be as easy for No.17 as I did not have a visit to the island planned, but fortunately a colour sample was sent to me by

the kind gentlemen of the Douglas paint shop.

It was going to have to be a mixing job, one of those little irritations the modeller of independent railways has to endure.

The finish on the model was made up from Revell ref.364, Humbrol 'Lemon Yellow', and a very small amount of Precision Paints 'LNER Doncaster Green', matched up to the colour sample.

Between 1992 and 2003 when in Brunswick green ex-works condition, the loco chassis had a bright red underframe and buffer beams. During its 2003 repaint only the buffer beams were treated, so the rest has been left to weather to a pink-red. For this I have used Humbrol no.60 but I have not faded it.

I am not sure why I have finished it so clean and short of oil and dirt! Perhaps I wanted to give it an appearance that was just that little bit newer than the steam fleet. The cowcatchers appear only ever appear to catch gravel and ballast; I have never seen these fittings without some sort of muck or dirt being carried around on them - a must for the model!

My only regret is that I wish I had never started hand lining my stock with a brush - there are too many straight lines on this one!

For the 'modern image' IoMR modeller this loco is a must, and I have to say it has grown on me. It looks very different and adds interest, shunting stock around Douglas, hauling permanent way trains, and even in charge of the odd passenger train.

Above: the completed chassis with brass spacers soldered in to hold the frame plates to gauge, and carry the motor. The exterior chassis details were made or carved from styrene sheet or commercial extrusions.

Below: the finished chassis assembly complete with the drive unit by Mike Chinery, which incorporates a flywheel. This was really designed as a power bogie for use with the Anbrico kits for the County Donegal railcars Nos.19 and 20. With a change of wheels and omission of the coupling rods, it suits the diesel loco chassis very well.

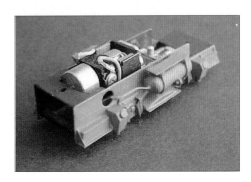

Initial stock – coaches

Coaches are mainly from kits by Roxey Mouldings, with a few from Branchlines (B).

F4 Guard/Third *Brown Marshalls 1876*
F8 Guard/Third *Ashbury 1881*
F15 Guard/First/Third *Brown Marshalls 1894*
F27 'Empress' van *Metropolitan 1897*
F29 Third saloon *Metropolitan 1905*
F35 First/Third saloon *Metropolitan 1905*
F39 Brake/composite *Oldbury 1897*
F44 half Third/Brake *Metropolitan 1908* (B)
F45 Guard/First/Third *Metropolitan 1913* (B)
F48 all Third *Metropolitan 1923* (B)

Coach F75

There is still room in 4mm scale Manx modelling for scratchbuilding - gaps do exist in the selection of available kits.

F75 is a rather special coach because of its historic value, individual character, and distinctive appearance. The prototype is still in existence and can be used, simply by pulling it out of the museum.

This coach has not always been used for special purposes, in fact right up to the mid-1960s it was in normal service on a daily basis. For this reason alone it fits in with my period.

F75 is known as the 'Governor's Coach'. It was made up from two of the original four-wheel coaches delivered in 1873: A12, which was used by the Duke of Sutherland, and C9, used by members of the Manx government. These two first class saloons were placed together on a bogie chassis in 1926. Both had deep blue upholstery, gilt paintwork, and polished woodwork including four carved folding leaf tables. They remaining separate internally until 1967 when a corridor opening was made,

and the upholstery was changed to maroon. The two inner tables were removed at this time.

As I had no drawings, the only thing to do was measure the real thing to obtain enough measurements and photos to construct the model out of plasticard and brass.

The body has much fine panel beading so plasticard was considered best for that.

A start was made on the chassis which was made easier by the fact that I had a spare Roxey Mouldings coach chassis of the correct dimensions with plate frame bogies.

At this point the monthly *009 News* reported that Alan Doherty of Worsley Works could produce an etched brass body kit to order if provided with suitable drawings and photos. So I sent off my drawings and photos. The kit duly came back, superbly etched. Worsley Works call their products 'scratch aids' as they provide the basic body shell and the basis of a chassis. The rest is up to the modeller.

I put the original chassis aside for another day, but did use the Roxey bogies, although

Worsley Works do now offer bogies separately. The new chassis was extremely easy to put together.

There is still a lot for the builder to put into this model to finish it. Footboard hangers need to be made from the side of the fret. No bogie mount or pivot hole is provided, so accurate measurement is required to make a fixing on the underside of the chassis, not forgetting to solder a nut inside for the bolt to hold the bogies!

I found it necessary to use plenty of solder on the chassis joints as the brass is quite thin.

The same applies to the body, so the long sides have to be treated with some respect. Once the four corners are soldered up it is advisable to add some extra brass to strengthen the whole thing.

Neither door handles or grab rails are supplied but holes are provided in the etching. Those door handles left from a previous kit are now invaluable! Handrails are made from 0.6mm brass wire.

As to the interior detail, I often research and install detail inside the coaches that allegedly

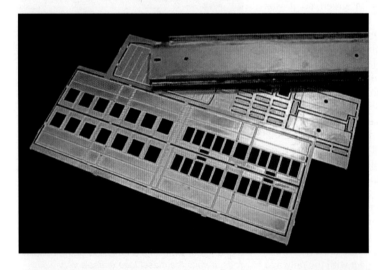

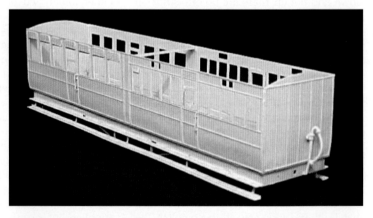

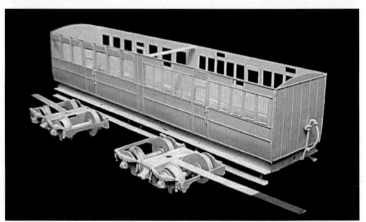

The Wickham trolley

I wanted to produce something just a little different for the layout, something out of the ordinary for a narrow gauge line. I remembered seeing the Wickham trolley at Douglas many years ago, and I thought it would be a suitable candidate.

This particular machine was not native to the IoMR. It was built in 1950 to 3' gauge for use on the Queens Pier tramway in Ramsey and was the property of the Isle of Man Harbour Board. It was loaned to the IoMR to assist in the refurbishment of the permanent way between Ballasalla and Douglas after the closures and short line workings of 1975 and 1976, and was scrapped by the railway shortly afterwards.

This project was not going to be easy, as I had no scale drawings. I calculated the width of the railcar using the 3' track gauge as a guide to the four equal sections between the side posts. This gave me a general idea of the scale and some basic drawings were produced. The most difficult task was to find the correct size wheels and a motor to fit within the outline.

The chassis was built of brass in the form of an oblong frame, with wheel bearings and a cradle to carry the Mashima motor, which is geared to both axles. To ensure the model was going to work and look convincing, a card mock-up of the body was made and fitted to the chassis as a temporary measure.

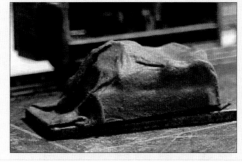

will not ever be seen. Whilst on the island I took many photos of the interior and noted the seat material used, how the tables worked, and ceiling detail. Some items have been altered over time, and some should be right for the period. For example, I knew some of the tables had been removed, but exactly when?

The interior was constructed entirely from plasticard to 1967 condition with the opening between the coach bodies. The movable cushion seating is pink/maroon painted card. All the walls, partitions, and tables are wood grained to as near as the real colour as I can achieve.

The roof is also plasticard, fixed on with Evo-stik contact adhesive. This coach has a large collection of mouldings attached to the side and top of the roof so care was taken to replicate this. Roofing felt is watercolour paper with two stitched lines down the middle to create the Stones lighting equipment. The wiring is covered by a plank on the C9 portion of the coach. The three wires are left to fix over the coach ends.

Colour is always an area of consternation, so I took colour swatches with me to the island to get the shades right but this only added to my problems because the red and cream on F75

was totally different to my swatches, and F35, the coach next to it in the museum, was a different shade altogether.

On F75, the cream was almost off-white and the red was almost maroon. I have absolutely no idea when this coach was last repainted. The only thing I can be certain of is that the chassis is black. So an assumption has to be made that it was repainted in the early 1960s when the interior was re-upholstered. *Port Foxdale* is set in the period 1960-1970, so therefore ex-works condition was chosen. The colours are Precision Paints 'Post Office Red' and Railmatch 'Early BR Cream'.

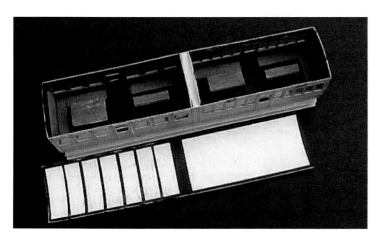

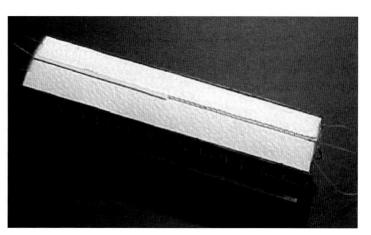

Above: composite F38 at Port Foxdale. The interior required particular attention.

Below: F38, built on the basis of a 'scratch aid' kit from Worsley Works.

F38

F38 is a six compartment composite, one of two bogie coaches built by Hurst Nelson for the Manx Northern Railway in 1899. They were very modern for their time and certainly above the comfort offered by any of the IoMR vehicles, and one wonders if the IoMR were rather envious of them. After the merger, they continued to serve the IoMR for many decades, and they must surely have been the inspiration for the large Fs ordered in later years by the IoMR from Metropolitan.

Both of these coaches are believed to be still extant somewhere in the UK but their condition is unknown.

The model of F38 was made from a Worsley Works 'scratch aid' kit, which provided two sides, two ends, and a basic chassis. The plush interior gives plenty of scope for some very intricate modelling.

The 'pairs'

It is now possible to purchase etched brass kits for almost all the IoMR coaches, from three suppliers - Branchlines and Roxey Mouldings, as noted above, and Worsley Works, who have recently produced in their 'scratch-aid' range the 'pairs', the 1873 four-wheel coach bodies twinned between 1905 and 1926 onto new bogie chassis.

The 'pairs' coaches are all much lower than the more modern stock, and together in a rake look magnificent.

I was lucky enough to obtain three very old GEM whitemetal kits of the IoMR four-wheel coaches. Two were cut up and had the integral chassis removed from the bodies so they could be placed on a full length bogie chassis, as running shortly after the combination had taken place with the gap between the bodies unfilled. It was duly painted in the post-1917 two-tone brown livery.

Van E5

E5 was one of the few early four-wheel passenger luggage/brake vehicles which, although dating back to 1873, lingered on for a considerable number of years. At least two were retained for use on goods traffic after their initial intended use had ceased.

Several of the bodies were removed from the wooden chassis and ended up as goods sheds in various places. E5 remained intact and was used as a store at Douglas station.

All these vehicles had disappeared or been destroyed by the mid-1970s.

The model was completely scratchbuilt out of plasticard, and has turned out one of my favourite vehicles. It is painted in the livery it carried in 1957.

(The prototypes and the model were fully described, with scale drawings, in the June 2004 RAILWAY MODELLER.)

Left: F35 and F36 had first class accommodation so my model of F35 deserved extra attention. Blue upholstery has been fitted with grained wood panels and pictures above the seats. Tram seats have been fitted to the third class section. The basis of the model is the etched brass kit by Roxey Mouldings.

THE ISLE OF MAN RAILWAY

Above: I was able to obtain three original Gem kits for the IoMR 1873 four-wheel coaches. These were stripped and rebuilt. I believe these kits were designed to represent the B class so one was built as it came but with the addition of wheel bearings and finescale wheels. Upholstery and interior detail were added. The exterior was kept complete with all the whitemetal mouldings intact rather than cutting them away and adding finer items such as handrails. The original balsa wood roof was also retained. Footboards and running gear are rather coarse but I did not want to alter too much of the old Gem kit. The coach was finished in the 1940s red-brown and numbered B11.

Top right: the ultimate design of IoMR coach has possibly to be the very unique and variable version of the 'Pairs' coaches. Several versions are now available in 4mm scale from Worsley Works.This variation is F68, formerly A9 (first class) and C13 (third class), four-wheelers paired in 1909. The desire to recreate the 1950s Peel school train required the coaches in the set to be painted in what was to be an extremely long-lived 'austerity' livery of red-brown. This could still be seen on some 'Pairs' in service up the 1980s.

Right: an IoMR E van from 1873, scratchbuilt entirely from plasticard. E 5 was probably the longest surviving member of this class of passenger luggage brakes. It was used as a stores shed in Douglas station for a number of years, retaining the 1917 tan and chocolate livery. This vehicle and many others were dismantled or broken up at Ballasalla in 1974.

Right: F27 'Empress' luggage van from a Roxey kit with light chocolate brown (Humbrol 63) upper section and dark chocolate (Humbrol 84) below.

Below: F44 is a Metropolitan half brake. The white square with red circle tail board on the rear of this coach was an introduction by Lord Ailsa to help bring the railway nearer to mainland standards with new rulebook workings. This coach is from a kit by Branchlines.

Below right: F39, the Foxdale coach, a Roxey kit.

Above left: one of the runners, created in the Ailsa period from a coach underframe when one of the 'pairs' was disembodied. A former British Railways standard gauge container has been placed on top and sits waiting to be returned to Castletown. The model was painstakingly lettered by hand.

Above: a small standard gauge container sitting on the quay at Port Foxdale. This represents one of the experiments by Lord Ailsa in the late 1960s to encourage freight traffic back onto the railway. These small BR containers were placed on M wagons with their sides folded down or the original 1936 well wagon. Hornby produce these mouldings in a set of four. All that was required was a coat of white paint, some home-made transfers to replicate the original markings, and weathering.

Left: the underframe of coach F54 as a bogie flat wagon in use as a permanent way runner, complete with brakeman. A brass chassis etching from one of the Roxey saloons enabled this vehicle to be produced, with the addition of the brake parts, plasticard wooden platform, and old rails.

Below left: M was not necessarily just for mineral, as anything went in these wagons - in this case, mine spoil from Foxdale.

Initial stock – freight vehicles

Most of the freight stock is made up from Branchlines kits. One of the advantages of these kits is that some very useful bits tend to be left over! These are great for scratchbuilding those odd bits of stock that were 'recycled' by the IoMR - oil tanks, container flats, and permanent way oddities.

5 x assorted M general purpose wagons
1 x H mineral wagon (modified kit)
2 x G vans (one converted as G19
     for use between railcars)
2 x K cattle wagons (one fitted with roof)
1 x E brake luggage van (scratchbuilt)
1 x permanent way bogie flat (F54)

The 'Man-tainor' is fitted to a scratchbuilt plastic chassis with Roxey bogies. The container is a Hornby standard gauge container, which took hours to paint and letter.

The Ailsa oil tank has a scratchbuilt plastic underframe (the prototype being a stripped M wagon) with whitemetal detail castings. A road tank from a plastic kit sits on old sleepers upon the wagon frame. Three of these very makeshift wagons were put together by the IoMR in the 1960s, and I will eventually make the whole rake.

Above: one of the H mineral wagons, although like the type M they carried anything, anywhere, anytime. Some of them were converted with planking to enable livestock to be carried.

Above right: a livestock wagon, often used for other things, such as hay or straw. In later years the insides were lime washed.

Right: a type G covered van.

Below right: three of these tank wagons were built in the 1960s as one of Lord Ailsa's schemes to promote freight traffic. They used M wagon chassis with road vehicle oil tanks resting on what seemed to be no more than old sleepers. Photos show the tanks painted in this bright orange. They were at some stage painted silver.

Couplings

When first built, all the stock was fitted with the very nicely etched scale Norwegian chopper couplings produced by Branchlines: these were, I thought, perfect, and matched the prototype. However, on the sharply curved track on Port Foxdale, the whole concept went awry, and all now have been changed to the etched Greenwich coupling.

Suppliers (4mm scale items)

Branchlines
P.O. Box 31, Exeter, EX4 6NY.
01392 437755
e-mail: sales@branchlines.com

Roxey Mouldings
58, Dudley Road, Walton-on Thames, Surrey, KT12 2JU.
01932 245439
www.roxeymouldings.co.uk

GEM Model Railways
101, Harrowden Road, Bedford, MK42 0RT.
01234 261481.
www.gemmodelrailways.co.uk

Worsley Works NG
19, Douglas Road, Worsley, M28 2SR.
www.worsleyworks.co.uk
narrowgauge@worsleyworks.co.uk

Greenwich & District NGRS
c/o 13, Rawlins Close, Addington, South Croydon, CR0 7AB.
Narrow gauge couplings.

Bibliography

The Isle of Man Railway (centenary edition) *J.I.C.Boyd*	Oakwood Press	1973	No ISBN
The Isle of Man Railway Volume 1 *J.I.C.Boyd*	Oakwood Press	1993	0 85361 444X
The Isle of Man Railway Volume 2 *J.I.C.Boyd*	Oakwood Press	1994	0 85361 4695
The Isle of Man Railway Volume 3 *J.I.C.Boyd*	Oakwood Press	1996	0 85361 479 2
On the Isle of Man Narrow Gauge *J.I.C.Boyd*	Bradford Barton	1978	0 85153 363 9
Rails in the Isle of Man *Robert Hendry*	Midland Publishing	1993	1 85780 009 5
Isle of Man Railway Album *R.Preston Hendry & R.Powell Hendry*	David & Charles	1976	0 7153 682281
Manx Northern Railway *R.Preston Hendry & R.Powell Hendry*	Hillside Publishing	1980	9505933 2 X
History of the Isle of Man Railway *Ian McNab*	Green Lake Publications	1945	No ISBN
British Railway Signalling *Robert Hendry*	Midland Publishing	2001	1 85780 114 8
Beyer, Peacock - Locomotive Builders to the World *R.L.Hills & D.Patrick*	Transport Publishing Co.	1982	0 903839 41 5
The Manx Peacocks *David Lloyd-Jones*	Atlantic	1998	0 906899 95 8
Introduction to Modelling the Isle of Man Railway *David Lloyd-Jones*	Warners/BRM	1996	0-9514144-3-7
The Isle of Man Red Guide	Ward-Lock & Co.Ltd.		
Isle of Man Tourist Brochure	IoM Tourist Board	annually	

Magazines

RAILWAY MODELLER	January 1988	County Donegal railcars Nos.19 & 20 (scale drawings by Ian Beattie)
Peco Publications	May 1993	IoMR 2-4-0T No.1 *Sutherland* (scale drawings by Ian Beattie)
	May 1995	IoMR 0-6-0T No.15 *Caledonia* (scale drawings by Ian Beattie)
	October 2006	*Ramsey* (OOn3 layout) by Alan Catlow (part 1)
	November 2006	*Ramsey* (OOn3 layout) by Alan Catlow (part 2)
	December 2006	*Ramsey* (OOn3 layout) by Alan Catlow (part 3)
	March 2004	1. The Isle of Man Railway - a modeller's inspiration
	June 2004	2. The permanent way
	June 2004	The E vans (with scale drawings by Jonathan Joseph)
	January 2005	3. Signalling
	January 2006	4. The diesel railcars Nos.19 & 20
	July 2006	Santon station - suggested layout (Plan of the month)
	November 2006	6. No.17 *Viking* - a German immigrant (with scale drawings by Andrew Beard)
	October 2007	7. Moving the modelling forward - additions to the layout and stock
		(This occasional series continues.)

Other useful sources

Manx Steam Railway News (Isle of Man Steam Railway Supporters Association)
Manx Transport Review
Ships of Mann magazine
www.manxnotebook (a useful website)

Acknowledgments

The late David Howard
  (formerly Director, Isle of Man Transport)
The late Colin Goldsmith
  and the workshop staff, IoMR
Paul Ogden, Isle of Man Transport
Roger Webster
Jeffery Kelly, Isle of Man Railway (retired)
The late Bobby Cowin
Mike Buttell
Port Erin Railway Museum
Grant Taylor, IoMSRSA
Lynda and Tony Beard, IoMSRSA
William Cubbon, IoMSRSA
Richard Dodge, Manx Electric Society
Manx National Heritage Library, Douglas
Museum of Science and Industry, Manchester
National Railway Museum, Library, York
Geoff LePage, Isle of Man Tourist Board
National Portrait Gallery, London
House of Lords Record Office, London
Institute of Civil Engineers Library, London
Real Paint & Varnish Co.
Ms Francis Coakley (www.manxnotebook)

Michael and Maureen Radcliffe
Dave Hammersley, Roxey Mouldings
Andrew Mullins, Branchlines
Allen Doherty, Worsley Works
Alan Catlow
David Lloyd-Jones
Tony Hill (photo collection)
Raymond Griffin (for help with the computer!)
David Warren, who was brave enough
  to read an early draft of the book
  and provided bus photographs.
All prototype photographs in this book are either by the author or from his collection, unless otherwise stated.
The black & white photographs taken by the late David Odabashian during the 1950s are from a collection he kindly submitted for use in RAILWAY MODELLER.
Thanks to Len Weal for the photographs of the *Port Foxdale* layout, as well as some of the loco portraits.
Other model photos by the author or editor.
Thanks to Brian Meredith and the Peco Studio.

Above: the frames and bunker of No.7 Tynwald *outside the goods shed at Castletown.*